KINGDOM WOMAN ARISE

Seize Your
Freedom and Destiny

Revised Edition
By Grace Cruz
Forward by Cynthia Yarbrough

ISBN: 1946106038
ISBN-13: **978-1946106032**
1st Revision December 2016

Glorified Publishing
PO Box 8007
The Woodlands TX 77387
www.GlorifiedPublishing.com

Dedication

I dedicate this book to my husband, Jose Cruz, who without his continuous love and support I would not have been able to accomplish many of my dreams. Thank you for being a strong man of God.

I dedicate this book to my three children: Aaron, Marisol and Marissa. You are my gifts from my Pappa God and I am very thankful for each of you and I love you unconditionally. I am very blessed to be able to say I have a family of believers in Christ and each of my loved ones have Eternal Life. I pray for you and bless you each and every day of my life.

Grace Cruz

Acknowledgements

I would like to thank and acknowledge all of those who have stood by me, have believed in me, and have supported me, personally and in ministry, with the vision God has given me. I want to thank Charity Bradshaw for mentoring me and helping to see my book project to the end.

I want to thank those who have been covering me in prayer, and all of my team members in Texas and Hawaii.

I want to thank my dad, Noe Cortez, and step-mom, Yvette Cortez for all of your continuous prayers and support. I want to thank my mom Sylvia for your continuous prayers.

Thank you to my dad, Noe Cortez, for being a man of God and covering me and my family in prayer every day. Thank you for speaking into my life and always encouraging me to be a Kingdom Woman. I Love you all!

Grace Cruz

Contents

Grace Cruz

Foreword

Grace Cruz is a true pioneer in the field of inner healing and deliverance, blazing trails in a ministry that is still difficult for some churches and church leaders to embrace. She has a unique gift and ability to draw people in and train them up in the things of God. Grace is transparent, using her own testimony to make plain the complexities of the deliverance process. She speaks openly about her own process as well as her years of experience bringing inner healing, deliverance, and freedom to countless others in this very exciting field of ministry.

God is moving in the deliverance ministry now more than ever before. As this ministry begins to regain its proper place in church today, often the key element that is still missing is the inner healing, or soul healing part of the deliverance process. Grace Cruz does a beautiful job of teaching us not only the various elements of the deliverance process, but she emphasizes the inner healing part of the process, which is really the biggest part if the process. She explains how the different parts of the process work together, and how inner healing is the key to the effectiveness of deliverance ministry as a whole. We all have soul wounds, and if we haven't addressed them specifically in an inner healing and deliverance process, they will follow us through the rest of our lives like a ball and chain. So if you have behaviors, issues, or soul wounds from the past that you've been pushing aside, or stuffing down because the church didn't know HOW to help you deal with them effectively, then this book is for you. If you feel called to the deliverance ministry, or are already ministering deliverance and want to learn how to increase the effectiveness of your ministry, then this book is for you. Let Grace Cruz share her insight and experience with you. You won't be sorry.

--

Cynthia Yarbrough

Pulling Down Strongholds Ministry, Inc.

Preface

Kingdom Woman Arise is a book that has been twenty-seven years in the making. It is the process I walked through to find my identity and purpose in life. It was not an easy life, but God loved me and He pulled me out of a deep, dark place to give me a new life. This book is about the process of going from the place from which He pulled, into a Divine destiny.

I truly believe that the process took so long for me, because I had to be knowledgeable of every aspect of the process I now call, 'renovation'. This is so that I could minister it, teach it and impart it to others. God had a plan to use my process, my testimony, to help others discover their freedom and destiny.

I pray that after reading this book, you will come to know, and understand, how the enemy works against you, and how to take hold of your God-given inheritance in Christ Jesus.

 - Grace Cruz

Note to readers:

The events that I write about are my personal experiences, and are true. They are how I view them, and how they have affected me personally. Others may have different opinions about certain events, but this is my story. After speaking and ministering to countless women over the years, I have come to know that all of our lives are similar. The strategies the enemy uses to bring down all mankind have never changed, and are still the strategies in use today. Evidently, the struggles I have had, many others have had also, because there is a familiarity, and a recognizable pattern. I have discovered that I can help others who are going through these same struggles. It is my passion and my calling.

Chapter 1

It's Your Appointed Time!

The Lord gives the command [to take Canaan];

The women who proclaim the good news are a great

*host (army); (*Psalm 68:11 AMP)

Have you ever felt that you were not living the life God intended you to live? Have you ever felt God has to have more for you? Are you sick and tired of living in lack, depressed, angry, and feeling as if your prayers are not being answered? Are you tired of the way life is treating you? Why are some Christians struggling, never able to be at a place of peace, joy or rest?

We have all the promises of God in His word. It is God's design, and His will, for believers to live in blessing and abundance. Why can't some experience this peace and abundance? What happened? This may sound as if I am whining and complaining, or being contradictory to God's Word. I am not. This is a very real place for many believers, and it's a problem for the church.

Many, including myself, had not been able to access and experience the promises of God in His Word. I know there are many of God's beloved people who are hurting, wounded, depressed, and living stagnate, defeated and ship wrecked lives. Too many are in this position, and have been for years. Many are born-again, church attending, Bible-study-going believers. This may be you. You have had a desire and hunger for the things of God: abundance, prosperity, peace, a life with purpose, and change - real change. Somehow it seems, there is something that is standing in your way, something that continues to pull you back into that same dark place. Every time you try to move forward one step, the enemy will pull you two steps back.

You may have tried for years and years to fight your way out of this place. You tried attending church, bible study, prayer meetings; you tried to do everything right; but, you have been trapped and unable to break through the walls, obstacles and pitfalls. I have been there and I have ministered to countless women who were in the same position.

The truth is you have an enemy. A real enemy, one who is unseen, who plans, plots, schemes and entraps God's people. This enemy comes to steal, kill and destroy you (John 10:10) and every good, Godly thing in your life. It is satan. He wages spiritual warfare against you. He has been waging spiritual warfare in your life, against the plans of God and against your inheritance in Christ, since your conception. His plan is that you never know salvation through Jesus.

When you become born-again, you become a daughter in God's family, and a soldier in the Army of God. You inherit every blessing and promise in the Word of God. The Spirit of God comes inside you, and you now have the fullness of God in Him, The Holy Spirit. There has been a constant, ongoing battle of good and evil going on in the spirit realm and it's personal. The battle does not end because you become born-again. In fact it becomes more intense. You are in it. You just may have not known it. You have been fighting your battles in the physical, natural realm. However, the reality is the battle is in the spiritual realm (Ephesians 6).

Now it is time to take your position in the Army of God, time to be armed and equipped with *spiritual weapons*, time to know your enemy and be aware of his schemes (2 Cor. 2:11). It's time to fight the enemy in the *spirit realm.* It is time to take hold of the fullness of the promises of your heritage in Christ, for you, for your family and for generations to come.

This is the motivation behind Kingdom Woman Arise:

The Spirit of the Lord is upon Me (the Messiah

Because He has anointed Me to preach the gospel

to the poor. He has sent Me to announce

release (pardon, forgiveness) to the captives.

And recovery of sight to the blind. To set free

those who are oppressed (downtrodden, bruised, crushed

by tragedy). (Luke 4:18 AMP)

God sent Jesus to pay the price for sin, but not only for sin. Jesus also bore the weight of sickness for healing: total healing of the mind, emotions and physical healing; prosperity in all things and from captivity of the enemy (satan and demons). God knew the fall of man would create bondage and give satan the upper hand over mankind, and, for this reason Jesus came; to destroy the works of satan in your life:

He who sins is of the devil, for the devil has

sinned from the beginning. For this purpose the

Son of God was manifested, that He might

destroy the works of the devil. (1 John 3:8 AMP)

It is my heart, more importantly it is God's heart, to see every person walk in the fullness of their inheritance in Christ. Too many of God's people are living under the power of demonic forces such as: depression, anger, hurt and pain, addictions, curses, sickness, fear, anxiety and so on. Yes, these are demonic forces that have come to steal your blessing and promise. It is my desire, and my destiny, to help you be set free through the healing and delivering power of Christ Jesus – to teach you spiritual warfare, to help you realize your true identity and authority in Christ, discover your purpose, fulfill your destiny and be the conduit of God's love and power. My destiny is to raise an 'Army of Kingdom Women Warriors' like yourself, who know how to defeat the devil. This is the purpose for the Kingdom Woman Arise books, conferences, teaching videos and webinars.

Burning desire

For many years, I have had this burning desire in me to write a book of my testimony and about spiritual warfare. The enemy brought pain and suffering which gave me a sad story of being a victim. Through God's amazing love and power, I believe that everything I went through, He turned around! He gave me the victory over the plans of satan, a powerful testimony and filled me with the power of the Holy Spirit and fire. God taught and trained me in spiritual warfare to teach and impart to other woman: how to be free from the influence of satan, and how to walk victoriously, in true freedom and power. Now, I am giving my testimony back to Him, to use for His glory.

I believe my testimony would be, and is being, used by God to bring transformation to lives of many women all over the world. I had visions of my story being much like many other stories, but through the grace of God my story had an amazing ending; thus, becoming a testimony. Unfortunately, not everyone's does. Had it not been for Jesus pulling me out of the hell I was in, the outcome of my story would have been death. I would not be alive today!

In the vision of writing this book, I saw that my testimony was a 'flame' that others needed for healing, restoration and transformation in their lives. God used all the traumatic, hurtful and bad experiences that happened in my life plus all the destructive choices I made, and turned them around into a destiny. He wants to do the same for you (Romans 8:28). I have been living a life of purpose by ministering to other women to find healing and freedom, by using my God ordained gifts, anointing, and power in the name of Jesus as weapons against the enemy. This is His divine destiny for me ... and the purpose of this book. I have been through the fire, and have overcome by the Blood of Jesus, and so can you (Revelation 12:11)!

I was not always like this. I had once been blind, oppressed, broken, downtrodden and captive; crushed by tragedy. If He did it for me, He will do it for you! Woman of God, if you have breath, then you have purpose. It absolutely does not matter what you have been through, no matter what you have done, or how far you have fallen, no matter what your skin color is, or what your economic status is, no matter what people have told you in the past, *you have a purpose*! It is God's will for you to be free, and walk in that purpose and destiny.

True identity

Daughter, your identity is found in Christ Jesus, what the Word of God says you are, and who He alone created you to be. The power to change your life is found in Christ, and in Him alone. I will walk you through the process, step by step, to get you on the road to your personal freedom and healing. I will help you to invite Jesus into your life, and allow Him to come into those areas where you have been crying out for real change, and for a miracle.

In *Kingdom Woman Arise*, I will share and give you the biblical keys and strategies that God taught me while going through the fire. Through His word and walking through the process, you will learn to overcome and live victoriously as a Daughter of the Most High God - a Kingdom Woman Arisen! The Holy Spirit is with you, and He will lead you and guide you through the whole process. He will speak to you, and reveal things to you in ways you never thought He could. I'm here to tell you, through the precious Blood of Jesus, you were bought with a price and the ransom has been paid. Kingdom Woman, it is your time! You *will* be victorious in this process, because it is God's will for you:

> *For even the Son of Man did not come to*
> *be served, but to serve, and to give His*
> *life as a ransom for many.*
>
> (Mark 10:45 AMP)

Vision

I remember one day I was very much at a peaceful place in my life. This was many years after the healing and deliverance process. Just out of the blue, I had been curious about something, so I asked God, "Why did I have to go through everything that I did? Why all the suffering and pain?" I remember I was lying down on the bed, waiting to hear from Him.

I fell into a light sleep and I had a vision. In the vision I saw where I had been hospitalized many times and I was on my death bed. Then, I saw Jesus walk into the hospital room where I was fighting for my life. I saw Him lean over and breathe life into me.

Then, I heard the Lord say, "I didn't want any of those things to happen to you, but, I was always with you. I heard when you cried out for me, I was there for you. I never left you. Now, my daughter I'm going to turn all of those things you went through into a destiny. I will lift you up. They will know you are Mine so that I may be glorified". I woke up with such an amazing peace all over me. I knew I had to follow through with this book.

Chapter 2

Identity, Purpose and Destiny

Your identity in Christ

'False Identity' is what many women struggle with. It was definitely one of the hardest things for me to overcome. I never understood that my past did not define me.

I conformed to being the things everyone else said I was, such as: circumstances surrounding my upbringing and the abuse that I suffered, the names others called me, the traumatic events leaving me wounded and broken hearted. I would go places, hoping I wouldn't run into people from my past, because it would only remind of my past.

The enemy was right there in my thoughts, reminding me of my short comings, never being pretty enough or smart enough, reminding me of mistakes and failures, assuring me that I would never live them down. I had a wounded soul and it blinded me from seeing my true identity in Christ.

It was when my soul was healed that it finally sunk in, and I didn't judge myself anymore, that I began to be free, and saw myself as God saw me. God really did create me in His image, and that is a 'sacred thing'. It was a miracle when I discovered my true identity. We have the fingerprint of God, you and I. How amazing is that? You and I are truly daughters of the Most High God. We are joint heirs with Christ Jesus…with Jesus! We are seated in the heavenly places! You, my sister, are seated in heavenly places. When you've never had a good identity of yourself, discovering the truth is transforming and miraculous.

Here is a word I received from the Lord while writing this book: The Lord is saying, "I am releasing power for supernatural 'soul healing'. I am breaking off false mindsets, old identities, healing wounds and the broken hearts of my daughters. I am creating in them a healthy soul. I am lifting them out of the pit of destruction and the miry clay, restoring what the locusts have devoured. I am causing increase of a thousand fold in every area of their lives.

I am removing the blinders from my daughters' eyes, so that they can see that I love them, and I have always been there for them when they cried out for me. It's time for my Kingdom Daughters to Arise! You are truly my daughters that I love with an everlasting love. You, my daughters, are seated in heavenly places. You are my *masterpiece*."

I really love the way the Amplified Bible version says this:

For we are His workmanship (His own master work, a work of art], created in Christ Jesus [reborn from above—spiritually *transformed, renewed, ready to be used] for good works, which God prepared (for us) beforehand [taking paths which He set], so that we would walk in them [living the good life which He prearranged and made ready for us). (*Ephesians 2:10 AMP)

If you have breath, you have purpose

The definition of purpose is the reason for which something is done or created, or for which something exists. Daughter, if you have breath in your lungs, you have a purpose. One of the things as humans we desire is to have a purpose in life. When God created *YOU*, He created you with a purpose in mind. It's already in you.

It was designed and built-in for all humankind. Your purpose is to live a life that brings glory to God the Father, to have a relationship with Him, to have fellowship with others, to live a good life and establish good works. If you are married, have a marriage that brings glory to God and a family that brings glory to God. Relationship with God matters above anything else.

Without a relationship with Him there is no real purpose in life. As a society, we've gotten so far away from living our lives according to God's purpose. Instead, we are living it for our own choices. Living according to our own choices causes us to live out of alignment with God's will.

Read: (John 15:1-17 AMP)

These scriptures clearly state that without God we are nothing, and without relationship with Him (abiding), we are without joy in our lives. This is why we hear of so many people achieving great things, but still feeling empty inside.

Most of my life I did not know that God did this, that He created me with a purpose in mind. Wow! Think of it…God Almighty was thinking of and you, just you. When we align our lives with His purpose, it puts us in a position for destiny!

Daughter of Destiny

I define destiny as a pre-ordained path for your life. God had a destiny for you all along. The enemy has come to steal, kill and destroy God's destiny for you. satan uses people and situations to blind you from your identity, purpose and destiny.

But now, it's time to step into, and receive, the healing power of Jesus and align yourself with your God-ordained purpose and destiny!

You may be thinking, "I have a destiny?" Yes! You were born with specific gifts: spiritual gifts, talents, anointing and a desire to fulfill a destiny here on the earth to advance His Kingdom.

God is releasing anointing, and opening doors of Kingdom ministry and businesses. He is releasing divine appointments, connections, finances, and strategically positioning you in this season. He has begun to release Kingdom books, social media mantles and creative ideas such as e-books, webinars, online schools, webcasts, Christian movies and much more to His Kingdom Daughters!

I also hear the Lord say, "I am delivering you from depression, fear of man, insecurity, inferiority and anxiety". As you are reading this just say, "I receive it in Jesus' name!"

Throw your hands up in the air and do a happy dance. This is good stuff! This destiny will be birthed out of a place of aligning yourself with God's purpose, which is to worship Him and glorify Him. I was no one special for God to have chosen me for His destiny. We are all chosen! You are chosen, because you are His. He created you in His image and He called you by name.

"Before I formed you in the womb I knew you (and approved of you as My chosen instrument),
And before you were born I consecrated you [to Myself as My own]; I have appointed you as a prophet to the nations."
(Jeremiah 1:5 AMP)

But now, thus says the LORD, who created you, O Jacob, And He who formed you, O Israel: "Fear not, for I have redeemed you; I have called you by your name; You are Mine. (Isaiah 43:1 AMP)

Called by name: A memory

I was at a prophetic meeting one day many years ago. This was during the time I was training for ministry. A woman gave me a word from the Lord. The Lord said that my name was no mistake. He named me Himself.

The woman did not know me, nor would she have known that when I was born my mother named me Gracie, but when she received the birth certificate it said Grace on it. She never changed it but she said it was a 'typo'. God said it was not a mistake. He marked me and He knew my name.

He knows your name:

11 For I know the plans and thoughts that I have for you,' says the LORD, *'plans for peace and well-being and not for disaster to give you a future and a hope.* (Jeremiah 29:11 AMP)

You are unique

The definition of unique is being the only one of its kind; unlike anything else; original. You are an original. There is high value on something original. You are valuable. You were purchased with the highest price. You are unique. You are one of a kind and you can love yourself and embrace your unique qualities. These qualities are what set you apart from everyone else. God knew exactly what He was doing when He created you.

You have a unique personality and voice. Everything about you is 'one of a kind'! I used to think I was awkward and weird. That was my false identity talking to me. I know now that I'm absolutely what I should be, and I'm incredible -- a complete package! I have the true identity of being royalty.

Spiritual Gifts

As Kingdom Women we have at least one Spiritual gift, but we can desire to have all of them, especially the gift of prophecy. It is important to study the spiritual gifts and operate in them, because we are spiritual beings. Yes, you have gifts given to you by the Holy Spirit. Believe it!

[4]Now there are [distinctive] varieties of spiritual gifts [special abilities given by the grace and extraordinary power of the Holy Spirit operating in believers], but it is the same Spirit [who grants them and empowers believers]. [5]And there are [distinctive] varieties of ministries and service, but it is the same Lord [who is served]. [6]And there are [distinctive] ways of working [to accomplish things], but it is the same God who produces all things in all believers (inspiring, energizing, and empowering them) (1 Corinthians 12:4-11 AMP).

Spiritual gifts are for all believers. This means you, Daughter! You have inspiring, energizing, and empowering gifts.

As for you, the anointing (the special gift, the preparation) which you received from Him remains (permanently) in you, and you have no need for anyone to teach you. But just as His anointing teaches you [giving you insight through the presence of the Holy Spirit] about all things, and is true and is not a lie, and just as His anointing has taught you, [a]you must remain in Him (being rooted in Him, knit to Him) (1 John 2:27 AMP).

This does not mean we do not study and learn from teachers, it is important that we are forever students of His Word and always learning from those who have gone before us. What this scripture is saying is the Spirit of the Living God is in you. He is the Holy Spirit, He is the Teacher and is in you. Stay close to Him. He will teach you, and guide you always, in every situation. You can trust in that.

Sister, Daughter, Kingdom Woman: chase after your destiny! It's a good thing! I have spent countless hours pressing and pushing toward what God has for me. It is the only true joy, it will give you purpose.

Grace Cruz

Chapter 3

You Are in the Army Now

Kingdom of Light vs. Kingdom of Darkness

One of the most common questions I am asked is, "How can a born again Christian be under the power of a curse, have sickness in the body or be demonized?"

Now may the God of peace Himself sanctify

you through and through (that is, separate you from

profane and vulgar things, make you pure and whole

and undamaged—consecrated to Him—set apart for His

purpose)*; and may your spirit and soul and body*

be kept complete and [be found] *blameless*

at the coming of our Lord Jesus Christ.

(1 Thessalonians 5:23 AMP)

The scripture states that we are a three part being: spirit, soul and body. Your spirit may be born-again, perfect and blameless, but the soul and body are *not* yet complete and sanctified. This scripture separates the three parts that all need to be worked on. Once you are born-again, your spirit is made perfect and you have eternal life. You have become born of the Holy Spirit, who is the Spirit of God, and the fullness of the Kingdom inheritance belongs to you. You become a 'new creation', to live the inherited life on earth. Your soul and body must also be made blameless. The enemy no longer has access to your Spirit, but he does wreak havoc on your soul and body, if he can. He uses the 'old things' to keep you from the 'new life'. The 'old things' are what I call 'legal rights' for the enemy to have an entry point into your life, creating strongholds.

*Therefore if anyone is in Christ (that is, grafted in, joined to Him by faith in Him as Savior), he is a **new** creature [reborn and renewed by the Holy Spirit]; the old things (the previous moral and spiritual condition) have passed away. Behold, **new** things have come [because spiritual awakening brings a **new** life].*

(2 Corinthians 5:17 AMP)

Satan comes to steal, kill and destroy (John 10:10) everything that is good and Godly, especially in the lives of God's people. That is what he does, and he is incapable of doing anything else. We are in a constant day-to-day battle with the forces of darkness, whether we are born again or not. Freedom from satan's curses and demonization can only come through Jesus. Satan is a legalist, meaning that he will take every opportunity, or what I call a 'legal right', to get a stronghold in your life.

This means that we must go through the process of 'renovation'. Even though the scripture says, "...the old things [the previous moral and spiritual condition] have passed away (2 Corinthians 5:17)", this is where too many believers get stuck, or what I call shipwrecked -- in the 'old things'. They become born again and that's it! They are still living their old ways, old wounds, old mind sets, old relationships, and old destructive cycles of living.

This is a place I am very familiar with. I was ship-wrecked for too many years as a believer, never being able to experience the fullness of my inheritance. I was never taught to go through the renovation process. The 'renovation process' is simply, but powerfully, the 'soul healing and deliverance ministry of Jesus'. A 'legal right' is defined as a fair claim, a legal claim, a vested interest, a legal power and authorization. In healing and deliverance ministry, a legal right is defined as something that gives satan a right to enter, to harass, to gain a stronghold to and in our lives.

Satan will begin his work as early as conception searching for a 'legal right'. The younger, the better for him, because, if he can get you young, you will have never known your true identity in Christ. Identity is very important to a person, and crucial to understand as a believer. It is the core of who you are. There are events in life that happen that shape a person's identity. Satan tries to make sure that those events that occur in life are destructive. Satan is predictable. He will try to do as much damage as he can, because his time is limited and there is no salvation for him.

God has laws in His Kingdom, and because we are His daughters and heirs of God, we have rights. Satan will always come to attack us. It's his nature, but He cannot get a stronghold unless there is a 'legal right' for him to do so.

These are nine 'legal rights' that allow satan to enter your life, to steal, kill and destroy your life and the lives of your children and future generations.

1. Generational sin and curses: involuntary sin bondage passing from one generation to the next generation

2. Occult involvement: past generations, present generation and personal entanglement. This includes witchcraft, curses and covenants, playing occult games Ouija boards, horoscopes, spiritual games and movies such as Harry Potter; light as a feather, bloody Mary, etc., séances, going to witch doctors, curandera and practicing witchcraft. By the way there is no such thing as a good witch -- it's all evil.

3. Abuse: mental, verbal, emotional, physical and sexual being the most destructive

4. Abandonment/rejection: rejection in the womb, a parent not being in child's life, divorce, abuse and neglect

5. Addictions of all kinds: drugs, alcohol, food, sugar, cigarettes, sex, etc.

6. Willful sin: voluntary sin that opens doors

7. Unhealthy soul ties: fornication, sexual abuse, incest, rape, molestation, unhealthy agreements, oaths and vows

8. Unforgiveness: roots of bitterness, resentment, holding on to offense

9. Strongholds of the mind: lies; reasoning, arguments, prideful thinking, false thinking patterns, false mind sets that have a fortified hold on your thoughts

A clean, proper, healthy soul will follow the will of the Holy Spirit, bring prosperity in all things, and bring divine healing for the body. A person with a dysfunctional, unhealthy soul will follow the desires of the flesh, opening the doors to demonization, sickness, and captivity. We will go through each one of these legal rights and remove them as you walk through the process of renovation (healing and deliverance) and following the guidance of the Holy Spirit.

I will not speak with you much longer,

for the ruler of the world (satan) is coming.

And he has no claim on Me

[no power over Me nor anything that he can use against Me]

(John 14:30 AMP)

Jesus means that satan, "shall find nothing in me" or "hath nothing to find in me". Christ had no sin in Him, which can be said of none but Him – 'but there is no judgment' or 'condemnation in Him' (see Romans 8:1). There is no cause for condemnation.

Though the accuser of men, satan, sought to have something against him - a 'legal right' - he could find none. Some pretenses were made, and charges brought, but the charges could not be made good; insomuch that the judge himself said, *"I find in him no fault at all* (John 18:38)," so that the devil had no power over him. He had no rightful power, because there was nothing found in Jesus for satan to have power over Him, meaning, no "legal rights".

You must walk through the process of removing any 'legal rights' so that there can be nothing in you that the enemy can use to bring death, sickness and destruction, or steal your prosperity, and the abundance that is your heritage in Christ. I know I keep saying this, but I really want you to understand -- it is your right and your inheritance as a daughter of the Most High God.

I am listing here some examples of what can happen to the three parts of your being by *not* walking through renovation, healing and deliverance, and *not* dealing with those 'legal rights' through the renovation process. The effects of these legal rights can be:

- *Spiritual Death:* never to inherit salvation
- *Soul Death:* unhealthy soul; a wounded, bruised, crushed and shattered soul; self-hatred, anger, rage, depression, mental illness, backslidden
- *Physical Death*: sickness in your body, infirmity and disease, premature death, death

Satan will take every 'legal right' to make sure that you are cursed, and living under the influence of curses, and in captivity. For me, it was at conception with the curse of illegitimacy, and then the curse of rejection from an unplanned, unwanted pregnancy. The next curse was incest and abuse. Those curses opened the door to more curses: fear, pain, despair, hopelessness, confusion, sickness, disease and infirmity, and suicide.

Those curses led to me opening my own sinful doors to destruction, anger, rage, unforgiveness, murder, death, suicide, lust, promiscuity, drugs and alcohol. All of the sin and curses intensified as I grew older, and had a stronger hold on me as the years went by. Satan made sure I entered into bad, unhealthy relationships. I would try to find something, or someone, to fill all of the emptiness and brokenness.

I was being sabotaged at every turn. He made sure I continued to be rejected as often as I could. That rejection continued to pile on, layer after layer. I couldn't see any other way, except through the eyes of rejection and fear. My mind was bound by 'strongholds' of false beliefs of who I was, what I deserved, and lies. Fear was the controller of my life, with lies and more lies.

I became manipulative, deceptive, and controlling and began lying, stealing and cheating. That was all I knew. That is how people treated me. They stole from me. They lied to me and manipulated me. I felt everyone owed me something. I was so lost and broken and shattered in my soul.

What I did not know was this: even though all of these things manifest in physical, natural forms, such as real people abusing me and hurting me, real physical sickness, and real emotional trauma -- it was all spiritual. Yes, spiritual. Satan and his demons are spirits, and they are the ones behind all of the destruction.

The Apostle Paul explains that our struggles are fought in the spirit:

Put on the full armor of God [for His precepts are like the splendid armor of a heavily-armed soldier], so that you may be able to [successfully] stand up against all the schemes and the strategies and the deceits of the devil. [12] For our struggle is not against flesh and blood [contending only with physical opponents], but against the rulers, against the powers, against the world forces of this [present] darkness, against the spiritual forces of wickedness in the heavenly (supernatural) places (Ephesians 6:11-12 AMP).

³ For though we walk in the flesh [as mortal men], we are not carrying on our [spiritual] warfare according to the flesh and using the weapons of man. ⁴ The weapons of our warfare are not physical [weapons of flesh and blood]. Our weapons are divinely powerful for the destruction of fortresses (2Corinthians 10:3-4 AMP).

God's plan

These scriptures clearly state that, as believers, we do not battle in the flesh. Our ways are different from the world's ways. Our weapons against the true enemy, satan, are spiritual weapons. If we continue to fight in the flesh, we will continue to live defeated.

A spiritual solider must have on spiritual armor and have spiritual weapons. She must be trained to fight in battle in the Spirit. God is Spirit, Jesus is Spirit and The Holy Spirit is Spirit. Only through God's love was it that He sent Jesus, His only Son, to the earth as man, to be crucified for the payment of our sin and the sin of every person that ever lived or will live. He was crucified, buried, descended into Hell took the keys back from satan, resurrected by The Holy Spirit, and ascended to Heaven. He now sits at the right hand of the Father.

Jesus is the only reason I could ever be set free, healed and made whole spiritually, physically and in my soul. Only through the blood that Jesus shed, for me and you, could we find true peace, joy, love, healing and prosperity in all things. Our battles are to be fought in the Spirit, with our spiritual weapons.

Jesus comes to give us life, and life abundantly (see John 10:10). Jesus came to destroy the works of the devil, so that we may have eternal life through salvation; but, also that we may have a prosperous and abundant life, free from sin and death. Jesus bore it *all* on Himself so that we wouldn't have to.

In this book, I will walk you through the process of healing your soul, *relentlessly* removing the 'legal rights' satan has on you to destroy your life, and pull down every stronghold. We believe for total healing and restoration in the soul and body, to break free of generational curses, to break the power of word curses, and ungodly soul ties. We will use our authority in the name of Christ Jesus to take your life back; to walk in the fullness of the blessed life, the abundant life, and the prosperous life God has created for you, your children and your future generations.

This is God's plan for you as a three part being:

- Spirit: inherit eternal life through salvation, perfect, carrier of God's love, glory and power

- Soul: prosperous soul, wholeness, peace, love, joy, submitted to The Holy Spirit

- Body: healthy, strong, long life, temple of The Holy Spirit, free from illness

This is turnaround time! Time for you to take your position in the Army of God as a warrior against the forces of darkness; to be free from the plans satan has for your life, your family, and your generations that follow. Matthew 11:12 AMP says, "*And from the days of John the Baptist until now the kingdom of heaven suffers violence, and the violent take it by force*". "Violent" in this scripture means to be eager and zealous. It is time to stir up the zeal of The Holy Spirit in you and take back your inheritance: peace, a future, hope, health, healing and prosperity in all things, and to walk in the plans that God created for you. You must choose Jesus, and take the path of freedom. You can do this. You must choose to be strong and courageous and battle the true enemy, satan:

[9] *Have I not commanded you? Be strong and courageous! Do not be terrified or dismayed (intimidated), for the LORD your God is with you wherever you go."* (Joshua 1:9 AMP)

Kingdom Woman, lay hold of the Kingdom of Heaven!

Understanding the healing process

I strongly urge you to start this process and finish the process with eagerness, relentlessly. Remember, the enemy does not want to give up his ground. He knows if you can be free, you will be a great threat against him. That is why he started his work on you in the first place, because he fears you.

Resources

Prayer and decreeing the Word of God are two powerful spiritual weapons against the enemy, so I have added decrees and a daily prayer to this book. I encourage you read them and speak them out loud everyday, along with pleading the Blood of Jesus and putting on your armor of God every day. I have used these strategies all of my ministry life, and they work! All of this can be found at the back of this book. Remember to do this every day. It will frame your world and align your mind with God's Word. You could also read my book of decrees, *Kingdom Woman Decrees for Shaping Your World*.

Each healing and deliverance chapter will include teaching and personal testimony. There will be Biblical strategy to receive healing and freedom. I also urge you to spend time in devotion and prayer with the Lord. This is a life change. In order to be free, these are the strategies you will need to maintain freedom.

Chapter 4

Background

Quote: "Sometimes you may struggle with your emotions. Unhealed emotional pain will lead to emotional suffering. If you are experiencing the emotions, then they are important! Pretending they are not there, will just prolong the suffering. Allowing your emotions to determine how you interact with life will intensify the level of pain and dysfunction you experience."

Story of my life - The junk that kept me bound in captivity

We all have a story. We all have a background: birth, where we were born, what our culture is, our heritage, various spiritual belief systems, sometimes even occult involvement. We have childhood events and milestones, teenage years and all that comes from childhood to adulthood; then comes our middle-aged and senior years. Regardless of who you are, you have a story. In-between those years, life happens, along with the events that take place in that life.

Unfortunately, not everyone lives a life that is joyful, healthy and prosperous. We do not get to choose certain things such as, our family, economic status at birth, and the events of our lives during childhood. We are born into it. Many children are being raised in broken and dysfunctional homes. The family mountain system has been broken, and this is reality. There is disarray in the homes of many families: a dysfunctional family, abandonment and rejection, parents leaving and abandoning children and families. There are traumatic and tragic events such as molestation, incest, addictions, abuse, violence, divorce and all forms of loss from it; loss of someone or something, maybe even a sickness, disease or infirmity that can be life altering.

We are experiencing world tragedies that affect every living person: tragic deaths, bombing, war, mass shootings, human trafficking, etc. These things really do happen, and they are very real. The effects of them are very real. Some stories are similar and some more traumatic than others. All traumas and tragedies have an effect on people, and affect different people in many different ways. The children of these tragedies and traumas become adults, who become captive, bound, wounded and brokenhearted.

I'm not speaking mainly about gloom and doom, sad and depressing topics. This is actually a book of victory and triumph, light defeating darkness; however, I need to paint this picture of the realities that can happen in a person's life, and the things we face as human beings.

In the first chapter, I mention that we are in a spiritual battle between the Kingdom of light and the kingdom of darkness. The Bible tells us to be armed, because the battle is not in the natural with flesh and blood, but with principalities, against powers, against the rulers of the darkness of this age, against spiritual hosts of wickedness in the heavenly places in the spirit realm (see Eophesians 6).

I will use my personal experiences as an example of battles. These are battles I fought in my life, both in the natural and in the spirit. This is not to dwell on the past, but in the hope I could give Glory to the Father for all He has done for me, through His love and power, in the name of Jesus.

Birth to Childhood

The circumstances surrounding my conception were not ideal or perfect by any means. I was illegitimate, meaning out of wedlock, and was an unplanned pregnancy. This opened the door for the curse of illegitimacy and rejection. The curse of illegitimacy is designed to work against a person's destiny, and the curse of rejection is designed to ensure that a person would live wounded and isolated.

I was raised by my mother and stepfather. I did not know for many years that my stepfather was not my biological father. The reason this is important to point out is, because it has to do with 'identity'. Believing who you are affects every area of a person's life. Speaking from experience, the only identity I had of myself was a false identity. I didn't feel as if I fit in and I wondered 'why'. I looked at myself as if there were something wrong with me. What I was feeling was the undercurrent of being a step-child. I know it's not like this in every home where there are step-children, but in my home it was like that. This was from my personal experience. I had always felt it.

I thought I was different, but not in a good way. I felt as if I were the least in the family, meaning I had the least value. I began to take on that identity. I looked at myself as less than everyone else at a young age. This followed me my whole life.

Identity to a person is everything. I will get deeper into the importance of identity later.

Family Belief System

Growing up, our family did not have any spiritual background, except that we were Catholic, and did not go to church. We even believed in other forms of false religion, such as reincarnation. I have a memory of sitting around with the family talking about what we thought we were in past lives, and what we wanted to come back as when we died, and reincarnated.

I remember females in my family would put an egg in a cup on the side of the bed when kids in the family were sick, believing it would cure them. As kids, we played occult, scary 'games', such as Light as a Feather and Bloody Mary, even Ouija board games, and speaking to the dead, which are really familiar spirits. Even though we were innocent kids, it opened doors to the occult, and witchcraft curses and spirits.

I later found out that many of my family members had visited witch doctors, and put curses on people - witchcraft curses. I remember my family visiting a Baptist church service, and we felt so uncomfortable. It was very strange to see everyone clapping and singing. Needless to say, we didn't go back. We were kind of all over the place when it came to what we believed, because our faith was not rooted in Christ. It opened a lot of doors to the demonic spiritual realm. I have another memory of my childhood of going to children's church.

Memory

My family members were party people back then, so on Sunday morning they would send us on the church bus that came around and picked up kids to go to church. I have memories of going to children's church services, and singing songs about Jesus. I would raise my hand every week to be saved, and at this church they held baptisms every week. So, if you got saved, you got baptized the same day. I did this every week. I don't recall ever knowing why I was doing it. I believe God used those people to plant seeds in my life. I was as young as five years old. God was working on me. I thank you, Jesus, for those children's church folks, and for those who ministered to us, planting seeds of the Kingdom in our hearts.

Abandonment and Rejection

Abandonment during childhood can affect a person all of her life. Abandonment can happen as early as in the womb, when a parent, mother or father doesn't want the child. Contemplating abortion can be a form of abandonment. Abandonment can occur when a parent works, too, or just simply doesn't pay attention, or spend time with the child. It can also occur when there is divorce, and the family is split apart. When a child is abused by a parent, it is also a form of abandonment.

The enemy will take advantage, and bring a spirit of rejection. Then the person continues to be rejected all her life. Walls of rejection are built all around. She sees life through the eyes of rejection and isolates herself so she won't get hurt and feel as if everyone is out to get her. This is real and destructive. Many don't even know they are dealing with this rejection; it is torment for the person living with this. It becomes a very strong hold on the person.

The five areas of abuse

These five areas of abuse cause the most emotional damage and destruction to the soul. It is important to understand abuse, and how it works in a person's soul, in order to tear down the structure of abuse, and receive healing.

Abuse is one of the 'legal rights' that are listed in satan's plan for destruction of our lives. As a child, I suffered every form of abuse: sexual, verbal, mental, emotional and physical. When *anyone* suffers any form of abuse, this will cause invisible, emotional and spiritual scars, which can be a constant aggravation and a stumbling stone in life. It will create strongholds or fortresses in the mind. Though it happened in the physical realm, its effects are in spiritual realm. This is a spiritual attack. This is an assignment by satan and his demons to steal, kill and destroy, and will open doors for demonization, no matter what age the victim.

Sexual abuse is the ultimate violation of a person. The sexual part of you, gender-wise, is who are as a person. The gender part of you is the identity that God gave you in His image. It is sacred. It strikes the very core of the nature of who God is, because you were created in His image. It's the most damaging offense when sexual violation takes place. It's the ultimate insult that will create more spiritual and emotional scarring than anything else.

There is a three step process to abuse that occurs, leading to bondage. When you are violated sexually, you are victimized, you are horrified, and you are traumatized. The sense of helplessness that a five year old would feel at that point creates the anger and rage that we deal with later in life. **Paraphrased from Bob Larson's article, "Five Areas of Abuse".**

As a child, you would have no idea how to process what is happening to you. This would leave the child hopeless, thus creating anger and rage.

This is what happened to me and many others; the Family Research Council in Washington, DC, which is a family oriented Christian organization, recently published an article about a survey that was taken in our churches. According to this article, roughly 40% of the people in our churches were sexually molested before the age of 17. Outside of the church, this figure is also about 17%. This tells us that hurting people are coming into our churches seeking help. If we don't help them, they will turn to drugs, alcohol or the occult for help.

Anger, rage, drugs and alcohol were ways of dealing with the trauma of sexual abuse. I won't go into the details of the sexual abuse. Everyone knows it's dirty, and if you've gone through it, you will understand on an even greater level. I was a little girl being threatened not to tell, even at gunpoint, or fear of receiving a severe beating. Fear came into me, and took over my life. I literally feared for my life. Many people ask why victims don't tell or ask for help. Fear! Fear can be a powerful force. They weigh the options in their minds. It seems as if keeping quiet is safer, because if you tell, then you will surely die.

Protection of the family was also an issue. The children do not want to be the cause of their family being torn apart. During those childhood years, I began to have nightmares, and sexual dreams that I couldn't understand. I had disgusting, dirty feelings. I am talking about six or seven years of age. I began to act out in a promiscuous manner, one not normal for a child. This promiscuity continued through my teenage and adult years.

I cried all time, especially secretly in the shower. I spent years doing this. The emotional pain and hurt set in, and became a part of me. This is the emotional scarring making a mark on my soul. I didn't understand why this was happening to me. I felt betrayed, because I couldn't say what I was feeling to anyone. Only as an adult could I understand what it was.

Children cannot run away so they push the pain down deeply, so that they are able to live a somewhat normal life. They begin to believe that somehow it was their fault, and live with the shame and guilt of it all their life. Many, many years later I was still carrying the spiritual and emotional scars of it. I became a victim, and I was a victim most of my life.

In past generations, sexual abuse was not something you talked about. If it happened to you, it was normal to take these hurtful, shameful secrets to the grave. The problem with that is the ugliness is allowed to continue into the next generation as a generational curse, and becomes more powerful with every generation, unless it is broken.

Emotional abuse can break a person, just as all forms of abuse. Emotional wounds can actually horribly break a person, and they will live life with literally a 'shattered soul', bruised and crushed.

The soul is not something that can be seen. These wounds can be devastating, and long term, without intervention. I never had intervention; my wounds grew larger as I grew older.

Effects of emotional abuse

Emotional abuse damages self-confidence and self-worth, resulting in low self-esteem, and magnifying issues of physical appearance and self-worth (identity).

Emotional abuse can result in trust issues; affecting and destroying relationships, and never being able to let someone get close, never feeling safe, causing recurring fallouts in relationships.

Emotional abuse results in feeling you cannot trust your own instincts due to undermining and manipulation from the abuser; convincing the victim that what she or he is remembering did not really happen. This is called "gas-lighting". Some people go into a state of denial, as if abuse never happened or that the abuse is not really an issue, downplaying the abuse.

Stress and physical effects can occur with long term emotional abuse, which can manifest itself as headaches, back pain, neck pain and problems in the extremities. I believe it can manifest sickness and disease as well. I suffered every single one of these effects of emotional abuse, even to the extent of severe pain in my back, neck and it spilled over into sickness and disease. All of these left me bedridden for many years, and in and out of hospitals, suffering, and on my death bed from severe Crohn's Disease and Ulcerative Colitis. These are triggered by stress and emotional problems.

These two diseases are incurable and debilitating according to medical specialists. I was completely devastated and hopeless in my suffering, without any hope of getting better. I felt as if I were being abused over and over, but through the sickness and disease.

It was so traumatic, that I did not want live any more. Thoughts of suicide tormented me for many years. I could hear the voices saying, "Just get it over with. You are not worth trying. It will be better for everyone if you just died. Just die, already". I thought of shooting myself many times. Thoughts of driving into a wall or off a bridge tormented me, but I never pulled the trigger. Something stopped me. I believe it was angels. Alcohol, drugs and violence were part of my life.

There are things that go on when you're around these things that children should not experience or witness. It can be traumatizing, and leave scars. It is an extremely unsafe atmosphere for children. I believe this is where the other forms of abuse came from, the verbal, physical and mental abuse. Alcohol and drugs can affect a person's behavior, causing them to be violent and abusive to those around them. When there is no one there to help or intervene, it becomes a scary place, and a fearful place. It left me passive and overly compliant. I felt I was walking on eggshells. I remember hiding in the closet. I didn't want to be the first one to be confronted by the abuser. I feared for my life.

The effects of verbal abuse on children include substance abuse, physical aggression, delinquency and social problems. The more verbally aggressive the parent, the more pronounced the problem. Parents, who tell their children that they are dumb, bad, etc., raise children who think they are dumb or bad and act as such (strongholds of the mind).

A study of physical health consequences of physical and psychological abuse concludes verbal abuse is strongly associated with chronic pain, migraine and frequent headaches, stammering, ulcers, spastic colon, frequent indigestion, diarrhea, or constipation along with many stress-related heart conditions. The psychological effects of verbal abuse include: fear and anxiety, depression, stress and PTSD, intrusive memories, memory gap disorders, sleep or eating problems, hyper-vigilance and exaggerated startle responses, irritability, anger issues, alcohol and drug abuse, suicide, self-mutilation, and assaultive behaviors.

The primary, or first, effects of child physical abuse occur during and immediately after the abuse. The child will suffer pain and medical problems from physical injury and, in severe cases, even death. The physical pain from cuts, bruises, burns, whipping, kicking, punching, strangling, binding, etc., will eventually pass, but the emotional pain will last long after the visible wounds have healed.

The age at which the abuse occurs influences the way the injuries 'or any permanent damage' affect the child. Infant victims of physical abuse have the greatest risk of suffering long-term physical problems, such as neurological damage that manifests as tremors, irritability, lethargy, and vomiting. In more serious cases, the effects of child physical abuse can include seizures, permanent blindness or deafness, paralysis, mental and developmental delays and, of course, death. The longer the abuse continues, the greater the impact on the child, regardless of age.

Emotional Effects of Child Physical Abuse

The emotional effects of child physical abuse continue well after any physical wounds have healed. Numerous research studies conducted with abused children as subjects have concluded that a considerable number of psychological problems develop as a result of child physical abuse. These children experienced significantly more problems in their home lives, at school, and in dealing with peers than children from non-abusive environments. Some psychological and emotional effects of child physical abuse include:

- Eating disorders

- Inability to concentrate (including ADHD)

- Excessive hostility towards others, even friends and family members

- Depression

- Apathy and lethargy

- Sleep issues – insomnia, excessive sleepiness, sleep apnea

Physically abused children are predisposed to develop numerous psychological disturbances. They're more likely to have low self-esteem, deal with excessive fear and anxiety, and act out aggressively toward their siblings and peers.

Social Effects of Child Physical Abuse

The adverse social effects of child physical abuse represent still another facet of the child's life influenced by the abuse. Many abused children find it difficult to form lasting and appropriate friendships. They lack the ability to trust others in the most basic of ways. Children who have suffered long-term abuse lack basic social skills and cannot communicate naturally as other children can. These children may also exhibit a tendency to over-comply with authority figures and to use aggression for solving interpersonal issues. The social effects of the child's physical abuse continue to negatively influence the adult life of the abused child. They're more likely to divorce, develop drug and alcohol addictions, and to physically abuse their own children. Adults who were physically abused as children suffer from physical, emotional and social effects of the abuse throughout their lives. Experts report that victims of physical child abuse are at greater risk of developing a mental illness, becoming homeless, engaging in criminal activity, and unemployment.

I can remember looking back at my life. I acted-out very badly. I was full of anger, rage, sadness, despair, confusion and revenge. I was on a road to destruction and no one knew it. There was no stopping this downward spiral of my life. My life had been planned out for me by the actions of others. Most people would look at me as a child who needed discipline, or a rebellious teenager, or as an adult who just made really bad choices, and couldn't forgive. I can recall people hating me because of the choices I made. I had absolutely NO CLUE the things I was doing were wrong. I was acting on what was inside me. I was just trying to survive and attempting to live life with a really messed up 'identity'.

I was very confused most of the time because I could not understand how my actions were bad. I saw bad behavior all around me; it was just life as I knew it. Yet, I was the only one being judged for the very things others in positions of authority around me were doing. I believe I was misunderstood. No one could understand the shoes I walked in. I didn't want this path. I certainly didn't choose it.

Alcohol, drugs and violence became a normal part of my adult life as well. I began selling drugs as a teenager at school. I was smoking pot as a teenager and drinking alcohol. I remember drinking beer at the age of five. It had been given to me by family members just because it was fun, and it was also a tool used as part of the sexual abuse.

I know there are many other traumas and tragedies that others go through, much worse than what I went through. Unfortunately, there are so many who are God's people, who walk around and live life in a haze, out of brokenness from abuse and trauma of many forms and do not ever get the help they need. Many go to church, and are not getting the help needed for true healing. There are so many who push it way down, and feel that if they push it down far enough, it will be as if it never happened. That is a lie of the enemy to keep you trapped and bound. I learned to hide it the best I could by keeping quiet, but I could not hide the effect of it in my actions and character.

If you have suffered any of these abuses, you're probably feeling a whole lot of emotions stirring up right now. What I want you to do is stop, pray, and then continue with this process. Continue reading and walking through the healing process. Jesus has made a way for you to be free from it all. He loves you, and He is with you, even now, at this very moment. I have been there and you don't want to live another day with the torment. Pray the prayer below, and also read Psalms 91. It is in the back of this book. It is okay to cry. You need to let the pain surface to the top to heal.

Prayer

Father, in the name of Jesus, I come before you today and I ask you to help me. Forgive me of my sins and come into my heart. You are my Healer and Deliver, My Lord and Savior. Father, I choose to forgive those who hurt, abused, abandoned and rejected me. I forgive _____. I break all soul ties with this person. I ask you, Jesus, to come into this situation. I give you all the pain of the abuse. I give you the hurt, fear and anger, the dirty thoughts and feelings. I don't want it. I ask you to fill those places with your spirit, love and peace. Give me healing and wholeness, in Jesus' name.

Pray this prayer as many times as needed, until you feel a release of freedom.

Footnotes:

www.domesticshelters.org

www.childhelp.org

www.everydayhealth.org

Bob Larson Article "Five Areas of Abuse";

All of the effects of emotional abuse were from articles on www.healthyplace.com

Chapter 5

Game Changer

After many years of living this torment in my mind, emotions and physical affliction, I continued to spend year after year in and out of hospitals because of all the pain and sickness in my body. I went through many blood transfusions to save my life, I had been so sickly. I was suffering. I mean really suffering. There was so much despair. I had no hope left.

Memory

I had been in the hospital for about three weeks when some people from a church came by to visit me. They said a friend had told them about me, and how I had been very sick, so they came to pray for me. I remember they shared Jesus with me, and I remember them specifically saying that Jesus could heal me. I kind of giggled, and laughed at them, because I thought people like that were weird. I was being nice, hoping they would just go away. So they prayed for me and they left. I do not remember how much time had passed before the next thing happened. I went out with some friends and ended up sleeping with a guy I knew from school. I had gotten very drunk. I was upset for some reason and drinking was my way of dealing with things.

Much like generations past, I ended up pregnant and unwed from that night. I was under a doctor's care, and I was contemplating my options of what I should do. I had a very strong desire to have this child and see it to full term. I consulted with my doctor and he was very upset, to say the least. He couldn't understand how I could let this happen. He said I was not able to carry a child to full term and I probably never would; my body was too weak and I was too sick.

I didn't know what to do, and it seemed no one else had any advice for me, which was really strange. I was devastated, but somehow the memory of those people that came to visit me in the hospital that one day suddenly came to me. I remembered they said I could call out to God, and He would answer. I went to my bedroom and closed the door and I got on my knees. I cried out to God for the very first time in my life. This is what I cried, "I need to know if You are real and if You can really help me. I need You to show me if You are real. Please show me, Please show me. Is it true what they said about You?"

At that very moment, I felt this peaceful warmth flowing from my head down my face and body. I heard a voice say to me I would carry this baby, and the baby and I would be fine. Then, I heard the voice say to stop taking my medications. I knew it was God I heard. I knew He answered, just like those people said. I knew I wasn't imagining all of this. I knew this was real, I had never experienced anything like this, and there was nothing to compare to it. I jumped up with joy and excitement. It was as if someone had given me a shot of instant hope! I shared the good news, only it wasn't as exciting to everyone else.

If you only knew how much medication I took, it was crazy for me to even think about stopping my medications. I made an appointment with my doctor to share the good news. I told Him that Jesus healed me, as if it were the most normal thing in the world! I felt as if I discovered some secret everyone else knew but me. I was so shocked by his reaction. He thought I was completely nuts! He said it was impossible, and he warned me that he was not going to be responsible for the tragedy that was about to happen if I attempted to have this baby, and stop taking my medication.

He thought I was going to die trying to carry my baby. He was an Orthodox Jew. I had no idea what that meant at the time. I believed my experience. I knew it was real, I never, ever doubted it was God.

I miraculously carried my baby boy to full term, even two weeks late; he was so healthy and had a full head of hair. He weighed 8 pounds. The whole time I took no medications. I had a reason to live. I found hope in Jesus for this first time in my life, and He chose to save me and my baby. There was a reason!

I started going to church and really loved it! I went to singles' group meetings, and prayed the best I knew how being a baby Christian. I was full-on running after Jesus. I dedicated my baby boy even though I was a single mom. I didn't care what people thought, I loved Jesus. It was a wonderful honeymoon experience.

On the flip side, there were still all the issues with bad family relationships that had not been dealt with, or healed. There were so many unresolved issues, and there was so much fighting and strife going on. I was learning how to be a mom with all of my bad background. I was constantly being told I didn't know what was I was doing, and I didn't. I was just trying to do my best under the circumstances. These are the very things the enemy uses as legal rights.

I began to feel hopeless again. The feelings of the pain and betrayal, and all the other horrible feelings I had before I was born again, began to surface. I started feeling sick again. The symptoms started coming back. Something was happening, and it wasn't good. Nothing I tried was working, and the pull was too strong. I began to be pulled away from God. I started giving up. I went into a complete backslidden stage.

What I didn't know then, but I know now as a minister, was that I still had so much 'legal right' for the enemy to cause chaos in my life. I had wounds in my soul, unforgiveness, generational curses, strongholds of the mind among others. I had not gone through the 'renovation', or 'healing and deliverance', stage of my walk as a believer. I began to use alcohol to cover the pain of my emotional and physical trauma. It was worse than ever before. At the time, I was being prescribed medications for pain for my back; I started mixing it with alcohol. It was good at the time because all the emotional and physical pain would go away, so I kept doing this. After a while it wasn't working, so I moved on to stronger things like other drugs mixed with alcohol.

It was my only escape. I became addicted to not feeling anything at all. At the time, it was a good trade off, until it took over my whole life.

I ended up repeating some of the things I had despised that other people did, mainly being in the drug world. I was surviving. I didn't know of any other way. I began to live the drug world lifestyle. In this world, drug dealers were respected, and I was tired of being the outcast. I was no longer an outcast in this world. I didn't think it was bad, because that is how I grew up. That's how I justified it – it was a stronghold on my mind, a lie that I believed.

I was so lost and clueless to reality, I had no true identity. My life's goal was to be with a drug dealer, live a fast party life and live happily ever after (stronghold). I swore I would never get married. My thoughts of marriage were horrible. In my eyes, all men were scum. I lived this life for the next eight years. During these eight years, I suffered and I was more bound than ever. My son suffered. He saw and experienced things no child should. I almost lost my life many times through sickness, drug and alcohol overdoses, or car accidents, people trying to shoot me, suicide attempts. So much tragedy happened.

There were moments where I would remember the powerful encounter I had with God, and all those times I went to the children's church. I would call out to Jesus, and make confessions like this, "One day You will rescue me; I know You won't leave me like this". Many times throughout the years I had confessed it. There was a small part of me that knew somehow it wasn't over, but it was a very small part. The seeds of hope had been planted and I was hanging on to any ounce of hope I had. The born again experience I had was very real, and the seed of Jesus was in me. I was fighting for dear life.

I want you to understand, I am no stranger to pain, suffering and tragedy. I went through hell and back, and then did it again and again, many times by that time. I am no stranger to fighting for survival. The battles I fought and overcame were through being in the trenches of personal experiences. I'm speaking to you from being there and fighting it out. I know some of you are still in this kind of battle. Maybe not with drugs and alcohol, but with the same soul wounds and curses that drew me to that lifestyle in the first place.

This is why I am writing this book and sharing my story, because you don't have to stay in that place. In the next chapter, I'm going share with you how this affected my married life. I know many of you will be able to relate. I minister to many women who have gone through the same issues, and are now walking in healing and freedom.

Testimony

I had been bound by addiction to drugs and alcohol, as if they were chains and shackles on me, and no one had the keys to set me free. I tried many times, but it was the deep emotional wounds, the pain, the hurt of sexual abuse and betrayal, unforgiveness from abuse, rejection and abandonment that kept me bound. Those were the invisible chains satan used to destroy me.

One day, I heard the Lord say, "It's time to come home". I wasn't sure that what I was hearing was the voice of God. Thinking about it awhile, I knew it was Him. I had heard that voice before in other encounters, such as, the first time I met the Lord on the floor of my bedroom asking if He were real; I was hearing the same voice.

I ignored the call from Him and continued with my daily life of survival, as usual. A couple of days passed, and I heard Him again, "It's time to come home". The voice was a little louder, and this time I replied, "How could you want anything to do with me? Look at me, and look at all the horrible things I've done. I'm no good to anyone."

I heard nothing and continued with my daily life. I knew something was happening because I discerned intensity in the realm of the spirit. I had always been very sensitive to the spirit realm. Another couple of days passed and I heard Him again. This time it was louder, and commanding, like an order. It was also wrapped in love. I knew He was serious. I could feel His compassion. He said, "Mija, daughter, it's time to come home".

I was so sure that He didn't realize what He was asking. I was certain He didn't understand I was too far gone for Him to want me. So, I rejected Him. I said "No" to God. I told Him I wasn't coming.

I knew at that very moment that had I broken His heart, because I left Him no choice but to take His hand of protection off of me. At that moment I realized, all this time, He had been protecting me from death. I cried out for Him to save me all those years, and when he came for me, I rejected Him.

Notice: He still called me Daughter and He was inviting me home. No matter what, He still loved me, and I was his, and so are you. He loves you with an everlasting Love (Romans 8:38-39).

Supernatural Deliverance

For the next three days, I experienced something supernatural. God opened my eyes to the spirit realm and I was able to see the demonic activity around me. I believe He was allowing me to see what I was choosing. I'm sure He was still protecting me from seeing more than I needed to, or more than He wanted me to see. I could see the demons plotting and planning against me. I saw how sneaky they were, and their hate toward me in their eyes. I could see familiar spirits, and snakes all over the place. I could even feel them in my body. I tried to get away from them, but there was no escaping the spirit realm. I could feel them trying to take my mind, to drive me insane. Somehow, I knew this is what happens to many people that lose their minds.

Many would believe this was a delirious episode I was having from drugs and alcohol but it wasn't. It was very real. On the third day, I was dying, literally dying. I felt the snakes taking over me, wrapping themselves around me, from my feet moving upwards. When they reached to my neck, the breath was leaving me. I was being asphyxiated by them. I knew that I knew I was dying!

I somehow understood that I was taking my last few breaths. I inhaled my last breath, and as I exhaled what would have been my last breath, I released it with a loud cry! I called out to God. I asked His forgiveness for rejecting Him. I cried out with such conviction, "I want to live and not die!" I began to confess, I wanted to see my son graduate and be married. I wanted to have a life, a real life and a happy life. "Forgive me, Lord!"

Instantly, in a snap, the snakes released my neck and I could breathe! I felt them leaving my body. It was so real that I lifted my shirt to look. I could see the faces of the demons spirits against my skin, they were being tormented as they were leaving and going down out from my feet. As that was happening, something else was happening at the top of my head. From the top of my head I was being filled with the Holy Spirit! It was warm, strong and powerful.

I was baptized in The Holy Spirit that day; there was fire all over me. I was coming back to life. I had been completely set free of an eight-year addiction to alcohol and drugs, with absolutely no withdrawals. Instantly my life was changed for eternity. I believe that is the day I was called by God, and anointed for the ministry I would be stepping into today. That was September 1998. I was glowing with the glory of God, set free by the power of Jesus. To God be the glory!

God anointed me to be a writer that same year. I finally finished this book, the one that I had been ordained to write, only to release in this time, September 2016, eighteen years later. I had been set free by the Blood of Jesus, because of what He did on the cross.

What was happening was that I had been set free from the addiction. The addiction was what the enemy had used to imprison my soul. It is what kept me in bondage. It had tried to continue to pull me into the darkness, and would not allow me to face my past, or deal with the abuse and all the other junk in my life. Being set free from addiction was a game changer!

Chapter 6

The light bulb turned on

Marriage and Family

I really loved my new life without addiction. I thought it was the answer to all of my problems, because it was on the forefront of what I was suffering. The truth was, I was messed up before the addiction, and now all of that junk was at the forefront. I still had much to learn. I had resumed my Christian walk as before. I started attending church, Bible study, and church functions. After all I really did love Jesus and that is the life I really desired.

I believed that the bad parts were over, and that I was on the road to true happiness. I was in a position to finally have a normal life, a "happily ever after", a life with Jesus. I started to have thoughts of marriage which was something I never allowed myself to have, because I believed all men were horrible and abusers, and because of what I had seen and experienced. I began to dream of starting a family, and owning my own home. I had thoughts of a church wedding, which was something I did not know I had in me. It wasn't long before I met someone. I heard the voice of The Holy Spirit say, "That is your husband".

It was one of those unexpected moments where the Lord surprised me. I really wasn't expecting it at all. This came to be a reality. I married the man The Holy Spirit said would be my husband. It was somewhat awkward adjusting to the idea of all of this. We dated and then were engaged. My soon to be hubby had a house built for me, while we planned our wedding. I had a church wedding, and there were over two hundred people in attendance. We had flowers, photographers, tons of food and three wedding cakes. It was beyond what I had imagined!

There was a part of me that was really happy with my relationship, and the whole blessing of having my desire of a church wedding. Deep within my soul, during the wedding and reception, I was in turmoil. I had an overwhelming feeling of shame, guilt and fear, and that I didn't deserve this amazing wedding, and everyone knew it. I pushed it down, and ignored the thoughts and feelings. That was a clue that I still needed healing, but at the time I wasn't aware of soul healing being a part of my Christian right.

I'm so thankful I have that memory of such a beautiful day. No one can take that away from me. I can look back, and I can appreciate my wedding and with everything that God blessed me. I can share that with my daughters. It's so awesome because they see the pictures, and they imagine a 'fairytale wedding'.

About nine months to a year passed, being married and living with my husband, I saw the joy slowly turned anger and distrust toward him. I thought when I was married everything that had been chaotic in my life would come to a place of peace. It came to be the opposite of what I had believed and expected.

What came to be true is that all the emotional trauma I had experienced as a child, a teen, and as a young adult, began to come up to the surface in my relationship with my husband. It was that junk again. Sound familiar? I had feelings of anger toward him that I couldn't understand.

No matter how much I tried to love him, all I could do was hate him. He wasn't perfect. I realized he had brought his own junk into the marriage as well, and his junk was irritating my wounds. It was as if he were sticking a knife into those places in my soul that had not been healed yet. Later, I had come to know this started because of things other men had done to me. He represented the men who had traumatized me during my childhood and other men who had abused me.

I was looking at my husband through the eyes of pain, hurt, abuse and abandonment. I was angry, critical and judgmental, controlling and overbearing toward my husband. I didn't know how to love him. I never really knew love, therefore

I was incapable of giving or receiving true love.

This was not a good thing for any marriage. My marital issues were piling on those other things I had already experienced. As a minister, I have found that this is happening in many Christian marriages, much of it coming from unresolved soul issues.

Another year had passed, and we started a family. We had two very precious daughters. They were miracles because the doctors said I couldn't have children. It was then, after the birth of my daughters, a light bulb turned on in me, something changed. I had a relentless desire to end the chaos and turmoil of my life for good, but I did not know how to do it. I did not want my children to grow up around a bad marriage where there was fighting, and a fear of losing mommy and daddy. I thought I had done everything I could possibly do and I knew God had supernaturally delivered me in a miraculous way, so I didn't understand.

I was more determined than ever to be free from all of this nonsense in my life. I was so tired of it My husband and I were fighting all the time; we grew extremely distant from one another. I contemplated divorce all the time. I began this inner battle of wanting to walk out on my marriage and wanting to ignore calling out to God for an answer.

I was devastated. Now I have a son and two very young daughters. This time I didn't want to die, or go hide out, or drown myself in alcohol or drugs. Something happened. There was a change in me, and something was rising up in me to fight. I could not let go of the dream I have had of a family and a happy life. I wanted to fight for my family and my marriage. I did not want my kids to suffer in a dysfunctional, or a broken home. I had a strong desire to save them from a life that I had suffered, but I didn't know how to go about it. I believe it was the seeds, and the supernatural encounters I had with God, that began to direct my heart toward God for an answer.

I turned my eyes to the cross, to Jesus. I believe it was the Holy Spirit rising up in me. I made a decision that I wanted it all. I remember confessing that many times over the years, "I want it all"! What I meant was I want everything God had for me and my family. I was ready to go to war for it. I believe this is when I began to take my position in the Army of God. I was transforming into a soldier and I didn't know it. It was another level of spiritual awakening.

Searching for more

I would cry out things like, "I'm tired of this; I can't take this anymore. I want something; I need something but I don't know what that something is. I know You must have more for me God. This cannot be it!" I knew that I knew that God had more for me. I was clueless as to what that was, but I knew it had to be better than what I was living, and I was clueless how to go after it. After all, I have had amazing, supernatural, miraculous experiences and I knew God was bigger. During this time, the pain in my body was worsening. I began to suffer in pain and agony, hunched over without being able to straighten up. Bed ridden most days, I no longer took prescription drugs, only 'over the counter' stuff. It was getting so bad that I had to go to the doctor for medication through injections. Meanwhile, I was in so much pain, the relationship between my husband and I had gotten worse because I couldn't function to be able to do things around the house and take care of the girls.

I was growing angry at my husband and my situation, and my husband was growing angrier with me. I grew angrier with him because there was no compassion. I began to feel victimized again. I grew angrier because I was sick and tired of being a victim. I refused to be victimized any longer.

Fort Worth Seminar

One day, out of the blue someone invited me to a conference in Fort Worth, Texas. I knew of the pastor speaking, and I knew he was a deliverance pastor. I had been to many of his conferences many years before, so I thought why not. I just felt a strong leading to go. I wasn't expecting anything for myself. I had no clue God was up to something.

Got the Revelation

I watched and listened to the seminar anxiously waiting for the pastor to minister to someone. It had always been amazing to watch the ministry sessions. So, I watched the pastor call a young man to the front to pray for him.

I watched as the young man shared his story of hurt and pain, of not having a father in his life while growing up, and as he continued to share, his hurt changed to anger, and this turned into full rage and murder. At this time, everyone was in tears. You could see the suffering and torment that this young man had gone through.

The pastor ministered to him by helping him to forgive his father for not being in his life, and walked him through the healing of his pain. Then the minister cast out spirits of anger, rage, and murder that tormented this young man, who was only 18 years old. You could tell he was a nice young man, just a statistic of life of whome the devil had taken advantage.

I watched as this young man became overcome with tears of joy, and thanking God. The young man was free. I was bawling in tears. I was witnessing an actual miracle, the love and grace of God. It was too much to handle. This time witnessing this type of ministry taking place had a completely different meaning. It wasn't just a cool thing to see, it was real. God became more real. His healing power became real.

My eyes opened to the power of God and the authority that has been given to believers over satan and darkness, in the name of Jesus; not only that, but the love of God for the hurting and wounded people. I had a revelation! This is what I needed. I stood up, thanking God in tears.

This is the answer for which I had been crying out to God. I knew it was real, because the young man that was being ministered to was my son. Yes, he was my son. It was God allowing me to witness the healing and delivering power of Jesus for my son. He did not want me to miss it. What a revelation! It was THE defining moment in my life!

We needed the healing power of Jesus. Not just physical healing, but soul healing, and deliverance healing power of Jesus! This was a transforming moment in my life. I could see the light. It's so crucial that we get this revelation. Too many pastors are telling Christians that Christians shouldn't have these issues, but we do. That is what the ministry of Jesus is about; healing the broken hearted and setting the captives free. (Luke 4:18)

After this Divine revelation, I made a decision to follow Christ. I already had salvation, but I'm talking about the 'more' for which I had been looking. It had just been made available to me, and my family, for the first time and I was going after it: the fullness of the cross. Nothing could stop me. In fact, there was no other direction for me.

This is what you can call a 'heavy revelation'. Once you have it, it's yours; no one can take it away from you!

The Renovation process begins

The ministry team that was ministering that day shared that they had a ministry team in the area. At that time, I was living in Waco, Texas, so it meant that I would have to travel one and one half hours to and from ministry sessions. That's exactly what I did, for two years, every Saturday, without fail, I traveled back and forth. Many in my family thought I was crazy and taking it too far, because I was missing out on family events, but I was on a mission for myself and my children to live the abundant life. The desire for peace, hope, joy, love and prosperity were the very things that kept me alive all those years. I fought and fought for my life, not even sure that I would ever have it.

There are much greater things than family events, such as freedom and heritage in Christ. Yes, family events are important but there is a season in life that we have to do what we have to do. It was everything to me, but at that time I did not have the full revelation of all that God was doing, only a small part of it.

While I had been going to ministry every week, I was receiving healing and freedom though Jesus, and learning about my true identity in Christ. I was manifesting demons and being set free. I was breaking generational curses. I was healing from wounds. I was being filled with the Holy Spirit and I was receiving spiritual gifts and anointing. The more I received the more I wanted.

I was expecting to experience Jesus like never before. I knew this was my time! In fact, on my second visit, I signed up for personal prayer, and the minister prayed with me. I grew very angry with him. All the anger from all of the abuse and all the times men hurt me and abused me came to the surface. This is what needed to happen. It could no longer stay hidden.

The minister prayed with me to forgive each and every one of those men. I renounced the spirits of anger, despair, anger of men, sickness and disease (Crohn's Disease), arthritis, molestation and incest. This was the day!!! I was free from it all!!

No more sickness, no more arthritis in my back, no more hurt and pain and no more unforgiveness in my heart. I was completely free from all of that once and for all, forever. The Holy Spirit came in, took those places, and filled me with Rivers of Living Waters. I was made alive!

There is a key to this. It was a curse. Forgiveness was the key to closing the doors to the curse of sexual abuse that set me free from the sickness. Once those things I had in common with the enemy's 'legal rights' were removed, the spirit of sickness and infirmity had to go. And did they go, fast!

Important Point

This is a very important point to bring to the light. The reason I continued to fall back into my old ways, even though I was a born-again believer,wherein the old things pass away and we become a new creation, was I had not yet gone through the renovation process of healing and deliverance which is a big part of Jesus' ministry. Jesus' healing and deliverance ministry is for the believers, to get rid of the old things. It is the right of every believer:

He was saying to her,

*"First let the children (*of Israel) *be fed,*

for it is not right to take the children's bread

and throw it to the [a]pet dogs (non-Jews)."

(Mark 7:27 AMP)

What Jesus is saying is that healing and deliverance is bread for believers in Christ, not for the unbelievers. This particular ministry is not made available or taught in many churches. That's a problem, because like me, there are so many born-again believers not experiencing the fullness of God, because there is no renovation process: cleaning out and ridding the old junk, pulling up the rug, facing your demons, cleaning out the skeletons in the closet. This is dangerous because this junk will come to make the believer then fall away, or stay stagnate, in a shipwrecked position, because they try and try to do all the steps of being a Christian and nothing is helping. They are the 'legal rights' satan uses against you. There is a saying we have in ministry, "Deal with your junk before your junk comes to get you!"

Having nothing the enemy can use against you is your heritage in Christ. This is what this book is about, the renovation process of getting rid of the junk that separates you from, and keeps you from receiving, your full inheritance as a believer.

I began to have thoughts of finding my biological father. I always wondered if I looked like him, and what he was like. So many questions were left unanswered, so many gaps in my life that I needed to be filled. I finally overcame the fear that always tried to intimidate me from discovering my true identity. I know my identity is in Christ, but knowing my father was part of my process to restoration. This was a major breakthrough moment for me, because I was free from fear, the fear and intimidation that controlled my whole life for far too long.

Chapter 7

Forgiveness

Key to unlocking God's miracle power

Before we start talking about forgiveness, I want you to know that this can be a very sensitive subject, because it may involve hurtful emotions of wrong-doing of others. Some of the content will be hard to swallow at first for some, but I'm going to pray for you, that you get through this chapter victoriously.

Father, In the name of Jesus, I pray for the woman, Your precious daughter, reading this right now, I ask You to cover her in Your wings and protect her from the enemy. I pray that You commission angels to take charge over her at this very moment, to minister to her. I pray that her heart is open to receive Your healing and delivering power, as she walks through the process of forgiveness. Lord, You know people have hurt and wronged her, and I know You do not make light of that. I know it won't be easy, but Your Word says that she can do all things through Christ, who strengthens her (Philippians 4:13). Help her, Lord. I thank You for what You're doing in her life. In Jesus name!

A little bit of facts

The Greater Good Science Center, based at University of California, Berkeley, studies the psychology, sociology, and neuroscience of well-being, and teaches skills that foster a thriving, resilient, and compassionate society defines forgiveness as a conscious, deliberate decision to release feelings of resentment or vengeance toward a person or group who has harmed you, regardless of whether they actually deserve forgiveness.

These are the benefits of forgiving according to GGSC

- Forgiveness makes you happier; forgiving can make you feel cheerful and joyful.

- Improves health; Unforgiveness can cause high blood pressure, spike heart rates, which are signs of stress which can damage the body. Forgiving causes stress levels to drop and therefore protects from negative health effects.

- Forgiveness sustains relationships: Studies show that forgiveness can stop a downward spiral of relationships and allows opportunity to repair before it dissolves.

- Forgiveness is good for marriages: Spouses who are less vindictive and are better at resolving conflicts, and forgiving spouses had stronger and more satisfying relationships.

- Forgiveness boosts kindness

These are all interesting scientific studies of the result of forgiving; now, let's take a look at what the biblical meaning of forgiveness is. There are two types of forgiveness in the Bible:

God's forgiveness of our sins and our obligation of forgiveness of others.

God's forgiveness

After the fall in the Garden of Eden, where Adam and Eve sinned against God, mankind has been sinning against God to this day. God, however, loves us so much that He took care of that separation from Him by sending His Son, Jesus Christ, to take our place on the cross, to be sacrificed for the *forgiveness* of our sin. Jesus did it. He paid the price, even though He was blameless. He took EVERY sin, even the most horrible of them, so, that we could be in right standing with God the Father. Did we deserve it? No, not at all, yet we are *forgiven.*

Thank you Lord!

"For God so [greatly] loved and dearly prized the world,

that He (even) gave His (One and)[a] only begotten Son,

so that whoever believes and trusts in Him (as Savior)

shall not perish, but have eternal life. (John 3:16 AMP)

Now, if we repent of our sins, and turn away from our sins and receive God's forgiveness, we are forgiven and have eternal life. Our relationship with God is restored. This can *only* happen through the work Jesus did on the cross for redemption of sin.

Forgiving others

As believers, this is the model of forgiveness you must follow. You don't forgive because the person deserves it. In fact we have a right to feel hurt when we have been wronged. You are human, but if you want to see God's miracles in your life, it is absolutely imperative that you **forgive**. We are under obligation to God to forgive others who have hurt us. The Bible is clear:

> *For if you forgive* [k] *others their trespasses*
> (their reckless and willful sins),
> *your heavenly Father will also forgive you.*
> [15] *But if you do not forgive others*

[nurturing your hurt and anger with the result that it interferes

with your relationship with God],

then your Father will not forgive your trespasses.

(Matthew 6:14-15 AMP)

[21] Then Peter came to Him and asked,

"Lord, how many times will my brother sin against me

and I forgive him and let it go?

Up to seven times?" [22] Jesus answered him,

"I say to you, not up to seven times, but seventy times seven.

(Matthew 18:21-22 AMP)

This may be hard to swallow for some because, understandably, some of the offenses are so hurtful, we can't imagine the person deserving forgiveness. I am by *NO* means undermining what was done to you, that it wasn't wrong.

You must understand that satan will use unforgiveness to entrap you with anger, resentment and bitterness. The lack of forgiveness can separate you from God. These are the very things that steal our peace, joy, health, prosperity, and freedom in Christ Jesus and the life that God intended for you as a woman of God. Forgiving means that you choose to release that person from blame, and put them in God's hands. Forgiving is for your benefit:

[13] bearing graciously with one another,

and willingly forgiving each other

if one has a cause for complaint against another;

just as the Lord has forgiven you,

so should you forgive.

(Colossians 3:13 AMP)

What will choosing forgiveness do for you

It turns you from a Victim to a Victorious Woman!

- Sets you free from the control of those you forgive.

- Close the doors to satan and any 'legal rights' he may have due to unforgiveness.

- Forgiveness can cleanse you and deliver you of resentment and bitterness; If you have never experienced being free from these things, I can tell you I have and it is miraculous. It changed my life forever.

- Healing for your mind and emotions: It is truly the freedom for which you have been longing.

- Healing for your body: Healing from sickness and physical pain.

- Release miracles and blessings toward you: Nothing can compare to what God releases in place of resentment and bitterness, they are heavenly blessing and miracles.

Through these two examples, you see forgiveness is the key, both in the natural and the spiritual realm, to living your life the way God intended. It is important to have God's forgiveness for salvation, and through that same salvation we extend that same forgiveness to others. I know your desire is for the peace and freedom of forgiving. That is why you are reading this book and have come this far.

My personal experience with forgiveness

My whole life, I viewed every situation through the eyes of the evil forces of anger, resentment and bitterness due to unforgiveness. I was a very defensive person and I felt everyone owed me, and everyone was out to get me. It was all due to unforgiveness. I had some very traumatic things happen to me as a child. I had suffered and endured all five forms of abuse, and I was angry at the people who hurt me, and those who didn't protect me, and those who judged me, and those who rejected me. I was filled with self-hatred, shame and dirtiness. I blamed myself and I was ashamed.

Through unforgiveness, hurt and pain spilled over into my body causing sickness and arthritis so painful I was unable to walk at a young age, which added more traumas to my life. I had done some bad things that I'm not proud of out of revenge, and hate, from unforgiveness. The things I did brought feelings of guilt and condemnation that I held against myself. I became uncontrollably self-destructive with no end in sight. I was completely lost.

One of the things I remember people would say to me is, "Just get over it", or "Grow up already", or "It's in the past; you have to let it go". Most times, it was not in love but in a judgmental way. I would get very angry at them. I thought to myself, "Don't they think I've tried? Do they really think I want to be this way?" This is probably the most hurtful thing to say to someone who is hurting and suffering with the torment of unforgiveness. Honestly, I just didn't know how to forgive.

I believe, today, you will realize the importance of forgiveness, and how it is a spiritual key to unlocking your freedom from a wounded soul and sickness. The 'legal right' of unforgiveness will no longer be available for the enemy to use against you.

One of the most important people to forgive is "YOURSELF". Forgiving and releasing yourself for all the things in your life that you felt you could have done better, or for the mistakes you made is a must. Let's face it, we all make mistakes. When you repent of your sins, God wipes them away forever; he does not even remember them, but sometimes we hold on to it, and there is no need. Forgiving yourself will free you from shame, guilt and condemnation.

"I, only I, am He who wipes out your

transgressions for My own sake,

And I will not remember your sins.

(Isaiah 43:25 AMP)

Therefore there is now no condemnation [no guilty verdict,

no punishment] for those who are in Christ Jesus

[who believe in Him as personal Lord and Savior].

(Romans 8:1 AMP)

Why people do not forgive

In my experience as a minister and through my own personal life experience these are the main reasons why people do not forgive:

- The person did not know they had unforgiveness
- Did not feel the other person deserved It

- Waiting on an apology

- Do not know how to forgive

In your eyes, these may be legitimate reasons not to forgive, because it involves hurt feelings of traumatic events and wrong doing by others. By no means are we to condone, or make light of, the actions of others that caused us pain and hurt. At the same time, this is not how the principle of forgiving was designed by God to work.

The model we use for forgiveness is God's; after all He is the creator of forgiveness. This false mindset toward forgiveness will keep you in bondage to anger, to resentment and bitterness, and possibly even cause sickness, disease or infirmity in your body. It will affect every area of your life. Lots of good people don't forgive, but there are consequences to unforgiveness.

Strategies about forgiveness to know that will help you in your process of forgiving:

- Unforgiveness grows and turns to bitter roots that must be pulled out by the process of forgiving.

- Forgiveness is not a *feeling*: hardly ever do we *feel* we want to forgive.

- Forgiveness *is a choice* to want God more than the unforgivenness, or the desire to be right. This is important to know, that it is a decision, and to separate our feelings from the offense. When I minister to people, I have them to declare this out loud.

Pray

Father in the name of Jesus, I _____, choose to forgive _____, as an *act of my will* and by *faith in God*, for the offense of _____, and I release them of any blame and now release them to you Lord.

I choose righteousness and I ask you to help me in this process.

There is no feeling involved in this. It is a choice to do as God commands in His word. Sometimes it's a struggle, so I have people repeat it until the mind and will come into alignment with what the person is confessing. It's a miracle to watch the look on their face when this happens and they align, and freedom begins to come forth; a real miracle.

Strategy 1: When I made these declarations for myself, I did have something in my heart; it was a desire to be free and to have every promise of God. I had to really dig deep into that desire to confess forgiveness at times.

Strategy 2: If you separate the person from the offense, as if seeing pictures, on one picture you see the person and on the other picture you see the offense, it will be easier to choose to forgive the person because at that moment they are not attached to the offense.

Strategy 3: Say out loud, "I choose to forgive, because God chose to forgive me first, and I choose to exercise my will as a Woman of God and to be obedient to God's Word."

Now, it's time to forgive those who *You* need to release. I know you can! Your Heavenly Father and all the angels in Heaven are cheering you on, and so am I.

This will take some time so you might need to be in a place where you're alone and it's quiet. If you are not, then you could read through it and come back to it a little later, but whatever you do, do not skip this step in the process; come back to it as soon as you possibly can. Make it your mission to forgive everyone!

Important things to know about walking through the prayer

- You will need to repeat this prayer for each person God shows you to forgive.
- It may be days later and you will need to come back to this prayer because He may reveal more people and sometimes it's just too hard to do it all in one sitting.

Before you get started, you should put on some praise music and grab a pen, you will need it.

Now you're ready. Put on your music, sit back, relax and ask Jesus to reveal to you who it is that you need to forgive. This may be a list, so write down who He reveals to you. He knows, so trust who He reveals. Ask Him for more. Ask 'why' if you don't know. God is faithful and will show you.

You may begin to cry and if so, go ahead say the prayer (repeat if needed):

Notes:

_____

_____

_____

_____

_____

_____

_____

_____

_____

_____

_____

Pray

My Father in Heaven, I come to you today with a humble heart and confidence, as Your daughter, that today I'm choosing to be free from the bondage of unforgiveness. I repent of the sin of unforgiveness, resentment and bitterness and I renounce these things from my life. I _____ choose as an act of my will by faith to forgive _____ for _____. I choose to release him/her from any blame and release them to You, Lord.

I break the ungodly soul tie with _____ and ask You to pull their parts out of my mind, will and emotions and bring my parts back to me, washed and sanctified in the precious Blood of Jesus. I ask You, Jesus, to heal me of all wounds as I give You my pain, and I ask that You deliver me from all the bad memories. I ask you to break all ties and cords to this person, I

111

renounce all sickness, disease, infirmities and conditions that came attached with unforgiveness and I command them to leave my body and my mind and my emotions *now*, in the name of Jesus. I give You glory, Lord, and I ask You to make me whole, in Jesus' name.

Footnotes:

The Greater Good Science Center website:

www.greatergood.berkeley.edu

Chapter 8

Soul ties

A soul tie is the 'knitting together' of two souls. It is a spiritual connection between two people who have been physically intimate with each other, or who have had an intense emotional or spiritual association or relationship. This can either bring tremendous blessing in a Godly relationship, or be a tremendous disaster causing destruction when made with the wrong persons in the wrong circumstances.

This is another one of satan's 'legal rights' to hinder your life. In this chapter, I am talking about past sexual partners.

I know this can be very personal and private. It's not to bring condemnation in any way whatsoever. This is only for freedom and healing purposes. We must know how the enemy works in order to be free from his schemes. One of the ways is through having sexual relations outside of marriage. I believe after reading this chapter, and walking through the steps, you will experience a whole new level of freedom and wholeness through the healing power of the Blood of Jesus.

The Bible does not use the word 'soul tie', but it does mention the 'knitting together' of souls. God created a 'soul tie' to be between one husband and one wife. The purpose of a Godly 'soul tie' is to create a deep-rooted bond. Marriage is the strongest Godly 'soul tie'. It is called a 'one flesh' bond. In the spirit realm you become 'one flesh'. When a soul tie is created with another person outside of wedlock, it can create unhealthy emotions in you. Anytime we engage in any form of sexual activity, it will form a deep-rooted bond.

A 'soul tie' is 'knitting together' of two souls: knit (verb) – to bind, to be in bonds, to wind, to tie.

When you're young, you think it's ok to have sexual intercourse, even though it's a short term relationship, maybe even one time. What's the big deal? Everybody does it. You might even believe the partner you are having intercourse with will be your husband one day, and then it doesn't work out.

The world makes us believe that waiting to have sex after marriage is old-fashioned or an out-of-date belief. But God created it that way for a reason. One, is to be pure and holy; the second is for protection from the enemy using the 'soul tie' as a 'legal right' to bring destruction.

Whether you are having sex with, or without, any feeling to a person, it creates an emotional and spiritual bond, a 'soul tie'. You may have had multiple sex partners outside of marriage. The implications of this are serious. While you think it is only a physical act, and once you break up it's over, that is the farthest thing from the truth. There is much more going on in the spirit realm on another level.

When you break up, or stop seeing this person, it is as if two pieces of wood that have been glued together are then forcibly pulled apart. Part of each piece of wood is left on the other piece. A piece of your sex partner, whether it's the good, the bad or the ugly, stays with you in your soul. The opposite is also true. Part of your soul stays with them, for the rest of your lives. You can only imagine what your soul looks like when you bond with multiple partners. The unhealthy 'soul tie' stays with you, and all of those persons' 'soul junk' is bound, woven and knitted to your soul for the rest of your life, until you receive deliverance and healing.

Soul ties and abuse:

Abuse, molestation, rape and incest also create an

unhealthy 'soul tie'. Consent does not change the emotional, and spiritual, bond that is created through intercourse. An unhealthy soul tie is a 'legal right' for the enemy. You may have opened the door through sexual intercourse outside of marriage (fornication). Having unhealthy soul ties is another strategy of satan to keep you in bondage, cause havoc in your life, steal your peace and joy, and hinder you from reaching the divine purposes God has for you.

How to identify if you have an unhealthy soul tie:

- Someone whose voice you hear in your head
- You take on the negative traits and offenses of another person
- Obsessive day-time thought about someone
- Dreaming or waking up at night thinking about someone on a regular basis
- Someone you think of or see in your mind when you are intimate with your spouse

- Cannot enter into a relationship because you still have feelings for someone in your past
- Go back to places that you had been with the person, hoping to see them
- Looking at past messages
- Picking up the phone wanting to call them
- Crying when you think about someone
- That person becomes like an obsession; to have to have that person back
- If the tie is from abuse, you many develop unhealthy feelings

None of what I'm saying is to judge you. I have been through breaking unhealthy 'soul ties', and though it was not fun, I did it because I want more of Jesus, and His promise of an abundant life. This is why you also must walk through the process of breaking 'soul ties'.

How soul ties affect your life

As a result, unhealthy soul ties can tie people's emotions and minds together by an unseen tie, cord or bind, creating a spiritual hold. I try to give a mental image of what this looks like when I minister.

This will affect and alter your mind, will and emotions, and even your personality. You may even act in ways you wouldn't normally act, because it is no longer just your own, but someone else's mind, will and emotions that are bound to yours. Then the two begin to think alike and make the same types of decisions, especially if they're not good decisions. I see this happen all the time in believers that come to church. I can discern when someone has 'soul tied' with someone else. It will show in their character, behavior and personality.

Picture this: how many people in your life time have you 'soul-tied' with that have altered your thinking, and your emotions, and even your will? Get the picture? We want to break all of these, and get you back to God's original design of who He created you to be.

Types of relationships

- Sexual relationships: fornication (adultery, sex outside of marriage), pornography, bad marriage
- Sexual abuse, molestation, rape and incest (penetration and non-penetration)
- Close non-sexual relationships: family, friends, co-workers, emotional affairs
- Spiritual leaders
- Agreements, oaths and vows

When any of these have occurred, you may be suffering from unhealthy 'soul ties'. I was living with an unhealthy soul for thirty-seven years. Eighteen of those years I was a believer. I am forty-seven years of age now. Some of you may be younger or older; thankfully there is no expiration date on God's promises, and healing and deliverance. There was a whole lot for me to clean out. When I had this revelation to clean house, I pulled out every cleaning supply I could think of, and went to work, relentlessly.

I mean, the enemy held nothing back. Even as an innocent child, he went after me so hard. I had to be just as relentless, and so do you. Meaning, I did everything I needed to do no matter how difficult; I just wanted freedom from the life I had always lived. Walking through this process was the best gift I could give myself, my husband, my children and all my future generations.

There is hope if you find yourself in an unhealthy 'soul tie'. You can never fall so far that you can't be restored. Freedom is available to you by simply repenting and asking Jesus to forgive you. Forgiveness restores the standard in our lives, and you can live in freedom and hope again.

How to break free

Thank you, Jesus, here we are! A prayer of repentance, and strategy in the all-powerful name of Jesus, can set you free. But, it will take time to walk through the many 'soul ties' that need to be broken. Sometimes, the emotions you might stir up with some of the ties can take time to work through, and that is okay!

The main thing is to take the step of taking back your life, blessing, peace and prosperity relentlessly, and do not quit the process. Keep going. You can do this. I'm cheering for you! This is not always a pleasant process. It may even bring back some unpleasant memories, but when you are finished you will feel free, and forever transformed. Freedom! That is your goal.

So, let's tighten our big-girl boot straps and do this! Grab a pen, read through each one of these instructions carefully, and as you are reading, The Holy Spirit will begin to bring people's faces or names to remembrance. You will need to write these names down so that you don't leave one out. You want to be thorough. If you cannot remember every name, Jesus will know and He will fill it in. Just do your best. Don't worry! This is for your eyes only. You can get rid of the paper when you have completed the process.

There are 4 Key steps to breaking soul ties:

1. Acknowledge

2. Confess and Repent

3. Forgive

4. Break and Remove

5. Restore and refill

Repeat this prayer for each person as The Holy Spirit brings names and faces to mind.

Soul Tie Breaking

Pray:

Heavenly Father, I ask forgiveness for the sin of fornication and sexual immorality with the following list of people, and those I do not remember, in the name of Jesus Christ. When I speak out their name and bring their face into my mind, and you forgive me, I will also forgive myself, allowing no shame, guilt or condemnation to come upon me or remain in me. I pray you would wash me and all my body parts in the

Blood of the Lamb so as to cleanse me and my mind. Please also, dear Lord Jesus, remove all memories of the sin as you restore me to wholeness.

Meditate: Ask The Holy Spirit to bring to mind every person with whom you need to break 'soul ties'. If you cannot remember their name (i.e., prostitute, or far back in memory) then say, "Lord you know who this person is. I break the soul tie with that person now, in the name of Jesus Christ." Work through each person slowly. Here is a sample prayer:

Pray:

I ask forgiveness for the sin of fornication and/ or sexual immorality with (name the person). I ask forgiveness for all the ways in which I hurt that person during our relationship and I choose to forgive all ways that person hurt me. Heal me in these areas now, Lord. I break all 'one-flesh' bonds and sever all soul ties, physical, emotional, mental, sexual and psychic. I ask, Lord, that all parts of me would come back to me now, washed in the Blood of the lamb, and I send all parts of them back to them, washed in the Blood of the Lamb. I pray also that you would now close all open doors or entry points forever in the name of Jesus Christ, including all objects of mine that they have and all objects of theirs that I have. I plead the Blood of Jesus over those objects removing all 'legal right' to harass me and I ask that you would pull out all sexual hooks from me and them. Lord, I bind myself to you and I ask you to make me whole and fill me with Your spirit. Fill me with all that you have for me.

REPEAT THIS PRAYER WITH EVERY PERSON THE HOLY SPIRIT BRINGS TO MIND.

Prayer for breaking soul tie from sexual abuse or rape

Father in the name of Jesus, I repent of all of my sins and I confess you as my Lord and Savior. I ask you, Jesus, to help me in this process. I choose to forgive (name the person), the person that hurt (abused or raped me). I release this person to you, Lord. I give you all of the pain, shame and dirty feeling of the act against me, and I ask you to take those places in me. Please heal me in these areas now, Lord.

I break all one flesh relationships and sever all 'soul ties': physical, emotional, mental, sexual and psychic. I ask Lord that all parts of me would come back to me now, washed in the Blood of the Jesus, and I send all parts of them back to them, washed in the Blood of the Jesus. I pray also that you would now close all open doors or entry points forever in the name of Jesus Christ, including all objects of mine that they have and all objects of theirs that I have. I plead the Blood of Jesus over those objects removing all 'legal rights' to harass me and I ask that you would pull out all sexual hooks from me and them.

Footnotes:

http://www.b4prayer.org/index10.html

Strong's Dictionary

DWJD Curse Breaking Prayers

Chapter 9

Generational Curses

What is a generational curse?

A generational curse is when someone in our past generations sinned against God, and opened themselves up to defilement; this defilement (generational curse) has been passed from generation to generation. The uncleanness is passed down, along with demonic spirits attached to it. As the new generations are born, they carry this curse. It does not matter that the new born child is innocent of any wrong doing. It is how things work in the realm of the spirit.

Ancestors opened doors and we are left to deal with the junk, in a nutshell. There is good news! Generational curses can be broken for eternity and the blessing of God can be released into your life and the lives of your family, through Christ Jesus.

Our fathers sinned, and are no more;

It is [a]we who have carried their sin.

(Lamentations 5:7 AMP)

The generational curse, or defilement, will cause the person to go through life struggling with what the curse is designed to do. It works against God's design for your life, and against your destiny in Him. Generational curses work not only against your life and destiny, but also your children's, and future generations' destinies as well.

The importance of breaking them is to **live the abundant** life promised in scripture (John 10:10); to be able to bear good fruit for the Lord; as well as ensuring the curse does not continue to pass on to future generations. Bringing glory to the Lord should be our greatest motivation to break curses. This is true. For me, living for God was *IT*, and there was no other alternative I desired.

The part of bringing glory to Him, was to bear good fruit in my family. My children were my next motivation. We want our children to live a life of blessing and have a Godly character. I'm not saying perfect children because, actually, there is no one who is perfect but Jesus. I'm saying create a heritage in Christ. Our heritage being to be fruitful, not cursed; to inherit our portion, our share of every natural and spiritual blessing and promise in God's Word.

Illustration of a generational curse: You see your children acting out in ways that you do not approve of, for instance acting out in anger, lying or manipulating. I'm not talking about just things that kids usually do as part of growing up. I'm talking about evil tendencies. You really don't like it, so you discipline the child, over and over, for the same thing for years even, hoping that one day it will stop. You may even begin to ignore it. You may even get frustrated and word curse the child by saying, "You act just like you father."

You're just doing what you think is right because you wouldn't intentionally curse your child. You just don't know what to do about it. It is because it is a spiritual issue, not a physical one. So you have to address it in the spirit realm. What you are actually seeing in this child is a generational curse in action, working its design against living and future generations.

This is a strategy I use to identify generational curses. I give my ministry clients this assignment: Go to a family event and take a note pad and pen. Pray and ask God to open your eyes to any 'generational sin curse' active in your family. Go back, watch and take note of all the things you see that are not according to the will of God. This includes actions, behaviors, addictions, even sexual immorality curses.

Those are the curses active in the family line. These generational curses have been active for so many generations, it has become part of the culture of the family. You may also find this in the culture of where your family originates, and if you have seen the same things going on generation after generation your family has developed a 'generational sin culture'. Another way to identify a generational curse is just to take note of any sickness or disease that runs in the family. It could be only in the females, or the males. It could be an addiction, or some kind of immorality, such as sexual immorality (incest, adultery, etc.).

⁵you shall not bow down to them nor serve them.

For I, the LORD your God, am a jealous God,

visiting the iniquity of the fathers upon the children

to the third and fourth generations of those who hate Me

(Exodus 20:5 AMP)

Yes, we are born with generational sin curses, but not all are activated at birth. Some curses have an age attached to it, meaning it will not activate until a certain age. Some curses will wait until the time of accountability, when the child is old enough to open the door to the curse. The word *visiting* in the above scripture means that curse will 'visit' in the sense of

131

making a call. The curse visits, or makes a call, but does not activate until the door is opened by another generation.

A curse will pull and pull, such as tempt and nudge, knock and knock for the next generation to open the door. So, when you are watching and taking notes at a family event, you will see mothers and daughters and granddaughters having the same behaviors and actions. The same goes for sons, fathers and grandfathers.

According to this scripture the next three to four generations are cursed. Three to four generations is the minimum; this curse will actually keep going until it's broken. Imagine how many generations are there in your bloodline, all the way back to Adam and Eve. There are just too many to count. Let's just say thousands of generations.

How many of those people sinned, or worshipped false gods? That's how many curses could be functioning in you, and your family, causing havoc and bringing death to every area it is designed to destroy. I'm not trying to discourage you, or overwhelm you, I want you to know and have knowledge, because knowledge is power.

Breaking the curse will stop the visitation for eternity. Wow!! Good news! God has given you authority to break them ALL through the Blood of Jesus!!

The circumstances surrounding my conception were not ideal, or perfect by any means. I was illegitimate, meaning born out of wedlock, and was an unplanned pregnancy (curse of illegitimacy). The curse of illegitimacy entered my life, but it didn't start there. This curse had been active in my family for generations.

Marriage after conception does not deactivate the curse. Illegitimacy means born out of wedlock. This curse and incest are the two curses in the Bible that affect ten generations. The effects and hindrances of this curse are: hindrance to worship, prayer, giving, reading of God's Word, and attendance at the House of God. Therefore, the curse will hinder being able to have personal relationship with God.

When we sin we curse ourselves, our children and our children's children and so on, strengthening the curses' hold on the family line to continue the curse for as many generations as possible, until one of those generations becomes the one to break the curse for all future generations. This is you!

Curses are not broken until they are broken

Generational curses are not broken automatically at salvation, when we become born-again. We discussed this in a previous chapter. You are a three part being: spirit, soul and body. At salvation, your Spirit is made perfect (regenerated), and you are saved from the law of sin and death. You now have eternal life, thank you, Jesus!

I can confirm to you, through my own life and countless ministry sessions where I have ministered to brothers and sisters that were born- again believers ... Christians can have, and suffer from, 'generational sin curses'.

Too often, we find this in many churches, and no one is helping others to be set free. Woman of God, curses are real, and they must be broken to receive the freedom and deliverance you're searching and struggling so hard to find.

A few facts about curses

- Not everything is a curse. Bad things can come through ignorance or stupidity, even physical causes.

- God curses: (Deut. 11:26) – blessings for obedience; curses for disobedience

- Satan curses – to bring death, destruction, and torment

- Intentional curses – something that you do or someone does to you

- Unintentional curses – one that comes on you from something that you were unaware carried them

- Causeless curse – (Proverbs 26:2.) It may be something that someone did to you

- Someone in authority over you opened the door and let it land on you. Almost every Christian suffers from this curse

- Robbing God in tithes and offerings! (Malachi 3:8, 9)

- All curses can be broken through repentance, and renunciation, and breaking the curse in the name of Jesus.

Who can you break generational curses? You can break curses off of yourself, your children, your husband and everyone you have authority over.

DEALING WITH THE CURSES

GENERAL CURSE BREAKING AND DENOUNCEMENT PRAYERS

Read it aloud. Make sure every word is said clearly and correctly. Also be sure to pray the daily prayer of covering and protection in the back of this book. Remember you have authority in the name of Jesus as a born-again believer.

Listen carefully: I have given you authority
[that you now possess] to tread on [1] serpents and scorpions,
and [the ability to exercise authority] over all the power of the
enemy (Satan); and nothing will [in any way] harm you.

(Luke 10:19 AMP)

Heavenly father,

In the name of Jesus, I ask forgiveness on behalf of myself, my mother and father and my ancestors back to Adam. I also ask Lord, wash and cleanse my bloodlines and that you would break all curses of these sins off me and my children, grandchildren and future generations following me. Also, please sever all soul ties as I denounce any spirits attached to these areas: false religion, pride, rebellion and witchcraft, rejection, anger/hate, depression, fear, death, suicide, murder, lust, sexual immorality, curses spilling innocent blood (abortion, miscarriage), isolation and loneliness, Jezebel/Ahab (control, manipulation, deception), addiction, new age, demonic amusement and entertainment (music, movies and games), false wisdom, infirmities, mental sickness and disease, biblical curses, curses from words (spells, word curses, gossip, slander), all sickness, disease and infirmity curses, and any other curses not mentioned here. I COMMAND by the authority given to me, in the name of Jesus that curses be broken off of myself, my children and all future generations and every demonic spirit attached to these GO NOW IN JESUS' NAME!!!!!!

You can repeat this as many times as you feel led by The Holy Spirit.

Breaking the curse of Illegitimacy

I, _____, confess the Lord Jesus as my Savior, and I renounce the kingdom of darkness. I renounce and repent of my sins, the sins of my mother and father and the sins of my ancestors back to Adam and Eve. I especially renounce the sexual sins such as fornication, perversion, adultery, lust, rape, molestation, incest. I renounce the curse of illegitimacy and any other generational curse that came into my family line. I break the curses and all effects and hindrances of those curses off of myself, my children and all future generations, in the name of Christ Jesus.

I ask you, Jesus, to release blessing in place of those curses, and to restore all that has been stolen to my family.

Footnotes:

http://www.deliverancenow.com/the-curses-of-sexual-sins/

Bob Larson, "Curse Breaking"

Chapter 10

Power of Words

Word cursing and blessing

When God spoke/speaks there is power in His words. The heavens and the earth were created by the spoken Words of God. He spoke them into existence, literally, with supernatural power. He blessed Adam and Eve with His words.

[3] And God said, "Let there be light"; and there was light.

(Genesis 1:3 AMP)

[27] So God created man in His own image,

in the image and likeness of God He created him;

male and female He created them.

(Genesis 1:27AMP)

The word 'tongue' is referenced many times in the Word of God as a spoken word (things that are said). The tongue reveals what is in your heart.

[8] *But whatever [word] comes out of the mouth comes from the heart, and this is what defiles and dishonors the man.*

(Matthew 15:18 AMP*)*

We also have power in our words, because we are created in the image of God and we are born of His Spirit. The words that come forth from our tongue (mouth) have the supernatural ability to bring forth life or death. When you speak life (positive, building up, loving, truth of God's word), it will bring life and blessing, and when you speak death (negative, putting down, cursing, harmful, lies) it will bring curses. Every person on earth has been affected by the power of these words; either positively or negatively or both.

Imagine all the words you have spoken in your life. How many times do you think you have spoken words that bring life, and how many times have you spoken words that bring death? Some things may come to mind right away, but there is no way to remember them all.

Try to imagine all the words spoken over you, or to you, that were life or death words, especially from parents, teachers, peers, even spouses. In this chapter, I will teach you what the Bible says about 'word curses and blessings'; how they come about, how they can bring destruction, chaos and harassment to your life; and how to break free from word curses and walk in blessing.

I had been a born-again believer since 1989, attended many Bible studies and discipleship classes, but never heard about 'word curses'. I believe, after you read this chapter, Kingdom Daughter, you will be free from the bondage of 'word curses' and you will understand more about releasing the blessing instead. You will also understand the power you have in your words and how to use them as a weapon against the enemy:

And I will bless (do good for, benefit)

those who bless you, And I will curse (that is, subject to My

wrath and judgment) the one who curses (despises, dishonors,

has contempt for) you. And in you all the families (nations) of the

earth will be blessed."

(Genesis 12:3 AMP)

This includes 'word curses' and blessings. Blessing and cursing work in two directions; people that 'word curse' you, and people that you 'word curse'. Let's face it, not one of us is perfect. I'm sure you have said some things that you wish you could take back. I know I have, and regret it deeply. There is 'good news'! We have the power to break the curses with our tongue, repent and ask forgiveness, and break the power of these 'word curses' through Christ Jesus.

"[8] But no one can tame the (human) tongue; it is a restless evil (undisciplined, unstable), full of deadly poison. [9] With it we bless our Lord and Father,and with it we curse men, who have been made in the likeness of God, [10] Out of the same mouth come both blessing and cursing. These things, my brothers (brethren), should not be this way [for we have a moral obligation to speak in a manner that reflects our fear of God and profound respect for His precepts). " (James 3:8-10 AMP)

How a 'curse word' works

This is the definition of a curse: A curse, like a prayer, is not a wish, but an invocation with expectation. The aim of cursing is to steal, kill and destroy. What happens is that someone speaks a 'harmful word' and, instantly a demonic spirit is assigned to those words, making it a 'word curse'. The evil spirit carries out the intent of the word until it's done, (the curse is in the intent of the words spoken) relentlessly, until there is a Godly, supernatural intervention, and the curse is broken and replaced with blessing.

These curses work in the realm of the spirit, in the unseen realm, because we are born of the Spirit. We also do not realize that some of the struggles we are warring against within ourselves are possibly the workings of 'word curses'. They could be working against you, your finances, your marriage, your children, your destiny, and your peace and your joy.

There are crimes that can be committed against you in the world, such as murder, rape, molestation, or theft. 'Word curses' are spiritual crimes, and weapons, that the devil activates or uses against you.

Junkyard Madness

If you are anything like I was, the enemy played a huge number on my life. As I shared in the previous chapters, I had a lot of work to do to get free from ALL the damage that had been done. I'll give you an example. My marriage in the beginning years was very difficult, to say the least. Jose and I struggled to get along. We were both in bondage and we both had 'junk' we brought into the marriage.

When I minister to women going through marital problems, I say this, "When both people who have 'junk' come together in marriage, you get a junkyard". That was us! I was dealing with the pain and the hurt of my past, he had a lot of anger and generational 'junk' he brought into the marriage. So, out of all of this 'junkyard madness', we cursed each other back and forth. Yes we did. Had I known the implications of it, I would have worked on changing my words sooner.

We knew that we shouldn't speak to each other in that way, and say hurtful, mean things, but no one had ever told us that those things we said out of anger and hurt would have an effect on our lives in the spirit realm, allowing demonic spirits to attack us and our children. Not only do they attack us, but they do not stop the pursuit of death and destruction until there is a Divine intervention.

'Word cursing' can start as far back as in the womb. I have ministered to many of God's people who had been cursed in the womb. Parents can say: "I wish I had never gotten pregnant. I wish this baby would die," or "I'm not ready to be a father," "it's not my child," or I'm having an abortion."

You may have grown up in a dysfunctional household where 'word cursing' each other was part of your daily life. If you did, then you know exactly what I'm talking about. We are human, and at the same time, we don't realize what we are doing until God reveals it to us, as He is revealing right now. As for me it was a long time before I had this revelation. Our adversary, the devil, doesn't care if you know it or not. He uses it as an opportunity, his legal right to steal, kill and destroy you and your destiny!

8 Be sober (well balanced and self-disciplined), be alert and cautious at all times. That enemy of yours, the devil, prowls around like a roaring lion [fiercely hungry], seeking someone to devour. (1 Peter 5:8 AMP)

"No weapon that is formed against you will succeed; And every tongue that rises against you in judgment you will

*condemn. This (peace, righteousness, security, and triumph over opposition) is the heritage of the servants of the L*ORD*, And this is their vindication from Me," says the L*ORD*.*
(Isaiah 54:17 AMP)

It is important to God to for you to vindicate yourself from words that have been spoken against you. He made it your heritage, a part of your inheritance. That is huge! God knew that we would need protection from all 'power words'.

At, some point in our marriage and walk with Jesus, Jose and I were made aware of how much we 'word cursed' each other, and exactly how satan was using these curses to destroy our marriage, children and future generations. The Holy Spirit revealed many strategies the enemy was using against us with 'word cursing'. Others were 'word cursing' us also, people we knew, and people we didn't know 'word cursed' us on a daily basis.

Have you heard the old saying we said as a child, "Sticks and stones will break my bones, but words will never hurt me"? It's not true, and not in alignment with the Word of God. The Holy Spirit also revealed that we have the power with our words to break 'word curses' and to release blessings. Blessings and curses are spoken. This is what we will be doing at the end of this chapter, but first I want to give you some examples of 'word cursing'. This will expose the enemy and his traps and schemes, give you empowerment, set you free and keep you free!

Examples of how husbands and wives curse each other:

- This marriage will never last.

- I hate you.

- I wish I never married you.

- I don't love you.

- I made a mistake marrying you.

- You are such a liar.

- You are such a nag

God knows the effect that words have on His children, and how the devil will take advantage anywhere he can find a way. These words work against your God-given peace, joy and prosperity. They work against what Jesus did on the Cross for your life. That is why many times in His Word God forbids gossip, backbiting and slander.

[20] For I am afraid that perhaps when I come I may find you not to be as I wish, and that you may find me not as you wish— that perhaps *there may be* strife, jealousy, angry tempers, disputes, slander, gossip, arrogance and disorder;
(2 Corinthians 12:20 AMP)

Let me give you some examples of how others, friends, strangers, family members, co-workers and teachers can 'word curse'. This may be through anger, jealousy, hate, gossip, backbiting or just plain ignorance:

- He/she is no good for nothing.

- He/she is an idiot.

- He/she will never amount to anything.

- You're so ugly/fat!

- Her/his kids will grow to be just like his/her dad/mom (cursing the whole family).

- She looks trashy.

- Shame on you!

- Are you Stupid? You're so stupid!

- She's such a witch.

- I don't know why he/she married him/her.

- I wish he/she were dead.

- You look like a clown.

- He/she is nothing but a failure.

- Four-letter 'word curses': F___ you! D___ you!

Curses you can speak over yourself:

- I'm always getting sick.

- I'm always broke.

- I never make enough money.

- Over my dead body!

- I'm always late.

- I'm always getting hurt

- I'm so tired.

- You drive me crazy!

- I can't.

- I should never have been born

- I'm always disappointing everyone

When a person in authority speaks a 'word curse' over a person, the curse is more powerful and more damaging in the spirit realm, meaning it carries more weight. The person in authority is actually giving the devil permission to put that curse into action. For example, a father, mother, grandparent speaks a curse over a child, a husband over a wife. Here are some examples:

- You're so lazy.

- You act just like your father.

- Shame on you!

- Can't you do anything right?

- You're such a pig.

- You never listen.

- Are you stupid or something?

All of these words the enemy takes advantage of, and assigns a demonic spirit to do his evil. By now, you should have a good idea about how we can be 'word cursed', and how these curses can affect our lives. Remember the scripture, "I will bless those who bless you, and curse those who curse you"? We can be on the other side of that by cursing others. That same will curse fall on us.

Truth

Curses land on the person who is to be cursed, but also lands on the person who speaks the curse. So, when you speak a curse, you also become cursed. When a person invokes a curse, they are making a contact with a supernatural being that has the power to inflict harm. So there is also a demonic spirit attached to a curse, and you sign on spiritually, in a contractual agreement with that demonic spirit, just by speaking the curse, which now has a 'legal right' to relentlessly work that same curse against you. This is good stuff! I am uncovering the schemes of the devil so can *you* be free and stay free from 'word curses' from this point forward.

I recently heard a teaching on the power of the tongue. It was a great message. The pastor executed the teaching well, and I believe many were changed to become aware of what comes out of their mouths. The people should be different from that point forward. However, I felt saddened in my Spirit because the teaching was lacking deliverance from 'word curses' from the past that were still hindering the everyday walk of God's people. They were still living in bondage from the words that had been spoken over them, all throughout their lives that would continue on to cause death and destruction.

God wants to bless you and He wants you to live in blessing. It is the reason He sent Jesus to do the work on the cross.   When God created the earth, He blessed it. When he created Adam and Eve, He blessed them. Abraham was blessed. (Genesis 12:2-3). Jesus spoke of blessing:

"Blessed (spiritually prosperous, happy, to be admired) are the poor in spirit (those devoid of spiritual arrogance, those who regard themselves as insignificant], for theirs is the kingdom of heaven [both now and forever).

4 "Blessed (forgiven, refreshed by God's grace] are those who mourn (over their sins and repent), for they will be comforted [when the burden of sin is lifted).

5 "Blessed [inwardly peaceful, spiritually secure, worthy of respect] are the [h]gentle [the kind-hearted, the sweet-spirited, the self-controlled],for they will inherit the earth.

6 "Blessed [joyful, nourished by God's goodness] are those who hunger and thirst for righteousness [those who actively seek right standing with God], for they will be (completely) satisfied.

[7] *"Blessed [content, sheltered by God's promises] are the merciful, for they will receive mercy.*

[8] *"Blessed [anticipating God's presence, spiritually mature] are the pure in heart [those with integrity, moral courage, and godly character], for they will see God.*

[9] *"Blessed [spiritually calm with life-joy in God's favor] are the makers and maintainers of peace, for they will [express His character and] be called the sons of God.*

[10] *"Blessed [comforted by inner peace and God's love] are those who are persecuted for [.]doing that which is morally right, for theirs is the kingdom of heaven [both now and forever].*

[11] *"Blessed [morally courageous and spiritually alive with life-joy in God's goodness] are you when people insult you and persecute you, and falsely say all kinds of evil things against you because of [your association with] Me.*

(Matthew.5:3-11AMP).

Glory to God that 'blessings' are part of the Christian life and faith. We should walk in the blessing.

So, now, let's get to work and break some word curses. Take a few moments to reflect on specific 'word curses' that the Holy Spirit reveals to you. These are words that have been spoken over you, and words you have spoken that need to be broken.

Prayer

Pray this prayer with authority, in the name of Jesus. Repeat this prayer as often as the Lord reveals more to you:

Father in Heaven,

I humbly come before you today. I lay myself before you as a living sacrifice. Search in me all 'word curses' working in my life. Father, in Jesus name, I choose to forgive, as an act of my will, by faith, all of those who have 'word cursed' me, my spouse or my children. Especially, the curses of _____ and all other 'word curses' I do not know about. I forgive _____ and release him/her to you to deal with. Father, include all 'word curses' that have been passed down our family generational line. Also, I repent and ask forgiveness for all 'word curses' I have spoken from my mouth against myself or anyone else.

I ask You to break the contractual agreements, oaths and vows I made with any demonic spirits as I spoke the words. I break the power of all of these 'word curses' from myself, my spouse_____, my children _____, all of my families' generations walking this earth, and all future generations. I declare that these curses are inoperative and ineffective against us NOW, in the name of Jesus!

I ask you to break any and all ungodly soul ties: physical, emotional, mental, sexual and psychological, with all of those who cursed me and those whom I cursed. I ask the Lord that all parts of me would be sent back washed by the Blood of Jesus, and send all parts of them back to them washed in the Blood of Jesus. I pray that You would close all doors and entry points forever, in Jesus' name!

Father God wants to bless you and He wants you to live in blessing. It is the reason He sent Jesus to do the work on the cross.

I ask You to restore back to me all that the devil has stolen from me through 'word curses', and I command that satan pay it all pay back seven fold, in Jesus' name.

Restore my marriage, my finances, my health, my family, my gifts and talents, my anointing and my destiny on the path that you have set for me. I choose to walk a 'blessed Christian' life, which is my right as a child of God.

Release the blessing on me, Father. I agree and declare that the power of the Lord Jesus Christ is all-powerful and effective to do this. I ask that my life fully magnify and glorify the Lord, in Jesus' name. Amen!

Chapter 11

Healthy Mind, Happy Life

Healthy vs. Unhealthy

We don't often think of what the condition of our mind is. Really, who does? But the fact of the matter is that as a Christian, the condition of our mind is a big deal. It's such a big deal that God references the word 'mind' 132 times in the King James Bible and 233 times in the Amplified Bible. It is because God speaks to us through our imaginations, thoughts, dreams and visions. In chapter two we discussed this.

1 Thessalonians 5:23 separates a person into a three part being: spirit, soul and body. The soul consists of our mind, will and emotions. Remember our spirit is made perfect at the time of salvation; it is in the soul that satan can enter to create a stronghold. In this chapter, we will focus on the part of the soul that satan attacks most - the mind. According to the Huffington Post, a person has between 50,000-80,000 thoughts per day. Every one of those thoughts is a seed, and those seeds have a potential to grow into something good and Godly. Or, if that seed is from the wrong fruit, it will grow into something harmful and destructive.

Our mind can be a thriving part of our spirit life, or it can be the very part of our being that satan uses to bring destruction to our lives. A spiritually unhealthy mind that has fruit with bad seed (thoughts) gives the enemy a lot of opportunity to create 'strongholds'. Our minds affect our thoughts, imagination and creativity. As human beings, we need healthy minds: physically, to be alive and thriving; and spiritually, a healthy mind that is in alignment with the Spirit of

God and is submitted to the Holy Spirit, bringing life and peace. Have you heard the saying, "I want peace of mind"? This 'peace of mind' we desire to have is rooted by setting your mind on things of the Spirit.

*For those who are living according to the flesh set their **minds** on the things of the flesh [which gratify the body), but those who are living according to the Spirit, [set their **minds** on] the things of the Spirit [His will and purpose].*

*Now the **mind** of the flesh is death (both now and forever—because it pursues sin]; but the **mind** of the Spirit is life and peace [the spiritual well-being that comes from walking with God—both now and forever];* (Romans 8:5-6 AMP)

What is a stronghold?

Satan will gain access to our lives by giving us negative and fearful thoughts, and incorrect thinking patterns. Strongholds of the mind are also known as lies, because they are the opposite of the truth, God's knowledge.

The definition of a stronghold is a place that has been fortified in order to protect itself against attacks.

(Synonyms: fortress, fort, castle, citadel, garrison, the enemy stronghold).

A place where a particular cause or belief is strongly defended or upheld.

The definition of a fortress is a military stronghold,; especially a strongly fortified town fit for a large garrison.

(Synonyms: fort, castle, citadel, blockhouse, stronghold, redoubt, fortification, bastion).

A heavily protected and impenetrable building:

A person or thing not susceptible to outside influence or disturbance.

[3] For though we walk in the flesh [as mortal men], we are not carrying on our [spiritual]warfare according to the flesh and using the weapons of man. [4] The weapons of our warfare are not physical [weapons of flesh and blood]. Our

weapons are divinely powerful for the destruction of for-tresses. [5] *We are destroying sophisticated arguments and every exalted and proudthing that sets itself up against the (true) knowledge of God, and we are taking every thought and purpose captive to the obedience of Christ being ready to punish every act of disobedience, when your own obedience [as a church] is complete (*2 Corinthians 10:3-6 AMP).

If I were to explain this in my own words it would be, "A stronghold is a fortified fortress in the mind made up of imaginations, arguments, reasoning, exalted and prideful thoughts; thought that are lies; negative, fearful and patterns of incorrect thinking".

Pulling down strongholds

'Pulling down' means to demolish, make extinct, and to destroy.

A Stronghold has three sides:

1. Arguments-an exchange of diverging views, clash, dispute, fight, reasoning, justifications.

2. Imaginations-speculations, deliberations, and fantasies.

3. Thoughts-the content of what a person is thinking. The process of holding something in your mind and rolling it over and over there.

A stronghold is built when we accept or agree with falsehood and lies; it forms in our mind as an imagination (a thought in our minds we believe is, and is not). How do you cast down this fortress of falsehood and imagination in your mind? We go to the Word:

[2] And do not be conformed to this world (any longer with its superficial values and customs), but be [a]transformed and progressively changed (as you mature spiritually) by the renewing of your mind (focusing on godly values and ethical attitudes), so that you may prove [for yourselves] what the will of God is, that which is Good and acceptable and perfect [in His plan and purpose for you].

(Romans 12:2 AMP)

It is clear that it is God's will for you to know what is good and acceptable, and what His perfect plan is for you. God knew that transformation would need to take place. He says to renew your mind. Renew means to renovate our mind: restore, rebuild, reform, alter, change, grow up, and strike through.

Renovation: to restore to a former, better state (as by cleaning, repairing, or rebuilding). Renovate by cleansing through the washing of the Word; our minds are transformed and strongholds are torn down. Spending time and meditating on the Word of God washes our minds and corrects our false thinking patterns (strongholds).

(Ephesians 5:26-27 AMP), *"[26]so that He might sanctify the church, having cleansed her by the washing of water with the word [of God], [27] so that [in turn] He might present the church to Himself in glorious splendor, without spot or wrinkle or any such thing; but that she would be holy [set apart for God] and blameless.*

Our warfare strategies:

1) As we meditate and wash our minds with God's Word, we will be transformed by the renewing of our minds; we will come to know the will of God, and discern what is right, perfect and good. Strongholds, which are based upon lies (false thinking patterns), will not stand a chance as the Light of God's Word (truth) is shed upon those areas of our minds. This is a game changer. You are no longer in the dark. You know the truth and the truth will set you free. (Ephesians 5:26)

Ephesians 6 gives us these keys:

2) I the Armor of God, 'the helmet of salvation' is the part that covers the mind is the helmet of salvation' (a spiritual covering that protects the head and mind).

3) I the Armor of God, the 'Sword of the Spirit' which is the Word of God will weaken and strike through and tear down the fortress by cleansing and renewing. This will be a process. It is progressive, and it will happen. You didn't get that way over night.

4)   James says to submit to the authority of God. (James 4:7)
Resist the devil (stand firm against him), and he will flee from
you. Submit to the Word of God (obey instruction), resist (stand
against, withstand, oppose) the devil (lies, false thinking
patterns) and he will flee; the stronghold will be demolished.
Halleluiah!!

Thank you Jesus!!

Encouragement and Prayer

The Holy Spirit taught me these strategies while going
through the renovation process. I would say this as a prayer to
get my mind and thoughts into alignment with God's truth.

Now, I continue to say this prayer, because it brings
continuous freedom. I teach it to my children. I don't want them
to fall into the same mind traps of the enemy. You can teach this
strategy to your children and grandchildren. So, with every
person, you will be creating a heritage and legacy of believers
who walk in power and authority, in Jesus' name. I urge you to

make this prayer part of your everyday prayer time as well as all the others in this book.

Pray

Father, in the name of Jesus, I repent for every agreement I made with the lies of the enemy or with any person. I break the agreements. I ask You to wash, cleanse and renew my mind as I mediate on your Word and resist the devil. I ask You to give me the mind of Christ, and let your thoughts be my thoughts. I thank you for grace and mercy and the blood of Jesus that washes, cleanses and sanctifies me every day, in Jesus' name.

Footnotes:

Google dictionary

www.livelearnevolve.com

Chapter 12

Decrees

You will also declare a thing, And it will be established

for you; So light will shine on your ways.

(Job 22:28 AMP)

The Word of God is true and infallible. When the Word says to decree or declare a thing and it will be established, it means just that. A decree is a powerful tool that will build the frame-work around your life. It will create what you decree for your life! It is also a spiritual warfare weapon.

The Lord says to decree a thing, and it shall be established. I am doing that very thing. I want to encourage you to declare these decrees over yourself daily. Decreeing will set God's angels into action to bring forth the manifestation of that decree in your life.

Bless the LORD, you His angels,

You mighty ones who do His commandments,

Obeying the voice of His word!

(Psalm 103:20 AMP)

Decreeing the Word of God is 'Kingdom living strategy and spiritual warfare strategy'. I hope that you will also begin to use this strategy as part of your everyday life, pass it on to your children and other women around you, and this will equip an army around you to be strong and mighty.

Decrees for you:

- I decree I am a Kingdom woman that walks in love and humility.

- I decree I am an overcomer and more than a conqueror.

- I decree I love the Lord our God above all else.

- I decree I am the righteousness of God in Christ Jesus.

- I decree I am washed and cleansed in the Blood of Jesus.

- I decree I am delivered and set fee from bondage.

- I decree I am blessed and highly favored.

- I decree I am prosperous in all things and walk in health and divine healing.

- I decree I am excellent of soul and my soul has nothing in common with the enemy.

- I decree I am a virtuous woman; a warrior in the army of God.

- I decree I am a woman who trusts in the Lord and will find new strength, I will soar high like an eagle, I will run and not grow weary, and I will walk and not faint.

- I decree I am fearfully and wonderfully made.

- I decree I am royalty, a Daughter of the Most High God.

- I decree I am a woman who fears the Lord

- I decree I walk in Your true identity, purpose and destiny.

- I decree I am a king and a priest.

- I decree I am an ambassador of Christ.

- I decree I am deeply loved by my Father in Heaven with an everlasting love

- I decree my Papa God cares for me.

- I decree I am His.

Identity Decrees

- I decree I am fearfully and wonderfully made.

- I decree I am created for purpose and destiny.

- I decree I am beautiful, unique and special.

- I decree I am a powerful Woman of God.

- I decree I am talented and gifted in many things.

- I decree I am I am created for signs, miracles and wonders.

- I decree my light shines in the darkness.

- I decree I am brilliant and I have the mind of Christ.

Increase Decrees

- I decree that I am blessed in the city and in the country.

- I decree I have the blessing of abundance

- I decree that everything my hands touch is blessed; I am the head and not the tail,

- I decree that I increase in boldness, strength, power and authority.

- I decree increase in prayer, intercession and intimacy with God.

- I decree increase in faith, hope and love.

- I decree increase in visions, dreams and revelation.

- I decree increase in anointing, gifts and talents.

- I decree many doors of opportunity are divinely opened for me.

- I decree that favor precedes me everywhere I go.

Spiritual Warfare Decrees:

- I decree no weapon formed against me or my family shall prosper.

- I decree every tongue that rises against me I shall condemn.

- I decree I am fully armed with spiritual weapons of warfare.

- I decree I am filled with the power of The Holy Spirit.

- I decree I will use my voice to decree and declare God's Word.

- I decree I resist satan and all his temptations.

- I decree I use and walk in my authority in the name of Jesus.

- I decree I will not grow weary in well doing.

- I decree I confess faith-filled words.

- I decree I am a warrior in God's army.

Esther Decrees:

- I am Esther. I have been called for such a time as this. I am blessed and highly favored. I am a chosen generation; a royal priesthood. I am royalty.

- I am Esther, I am a daughter of the King, I am a Princess through God's Royalty; crowned with His jewels, I stand knowing who I am called to be, and I am a joint heir with Jesus; through whom I am holy and righteous.

- I am fearfully and wonderfully made. I well know that God has a purpose for my life, plans to prosper me, and plans to give me a hope and a future in HIM. I am created in the image of God, and I have been set apart for greatness! I WILL fulfill my destiny!

- I am Esther. I have been predestined; I have been chosen. I am here for a reason, I am called to be a prophetess to the nations, and I am a carrier of His light to this world.

- I am filled with the fullness of God, and I am rooted and grounded in love. I am a carrier of His word, and I will set the captives free. I am covered by His love, and my time is NOW!

- I am prosperous in all things, and I will walk in the truth and in the way of He who called me. I am His delight, and I am predestined for His plan and purpose.

- I am more than a conqueror through Jesus Christ; I am an overcomer and one who walks in authority, knowing that I am victorious. I am a living testimony of His power and might!

- I am accepted. I am more than enough. I am of great worth. I am loved, and I will never walk alone. I am a daughter of God, chosen before birth.

- I have been established, anointed and sealed by God in Christ; I was bought at a price by Jesus. I am His workmanship. I am His masterpiece.

- I am an expression of the life of Christ because He is my life. I shall not die; I will live to declare the works God.

- I am Esther. Chosen for now, but God doesn't see age. I am chosen for such a time as this; I am chosen to be a voice for those without one. I am called to be the light of the world and the salt of the earth. I am called to be a carrier of the Word, and I will move in the power given me.

- I am Esther. I am created to praise God. I am not a victim of circumstances, but I am made stronger by them. I am not what man may say about me, but I am called for this very moment! I am chosen to lead a generation who is not ashamed to step up and step out! I am destined to take everything back that the enemy has stolen. I have dominion and power through Jesus Christ our Lord!

Daily Prayers

Covering and Protection

"Father, in the name of Jesus, I worship You, love You and adore You for all that You are, You are Good, Great and Holy. You are the Creator of the heavens and the earth and all things in it. I come boldly before Your Throne of Grace and I repent of my sins and I lay myself before You, a living sacrifice. Search me and cleanse me of everything unpleasing to You, Father, in the name of Jesus. Thank You, Father, that Your mercies are new every day. I thank You for every breath that I take.

I enter into Your gates with thanksgiving *and* into Your courts with praise: I am thankful to You and I bless Your name, I praise and worship You Lord.

I plead the Blood of Jesus over myself and all my family from our heads to our feet, the protecting, cleansing, healing Blood of Jesus.

I put on the full armor of God. As Your word says, "I put on the full armor of God, so that when the day of evil comes, I may be able to stand my ground, and after I have done everything, to stand. I stand firm, with the belt of truth buckled around my waist, with the breastplate of righteousness in place: with my feet fitted with the readiness that comes from the gospel of peace. In addition to all this, I take up the shield of faith, with which I can extinguish all the flaming arrows of the evil one. I put on the helmet of salvation and take the sword of the Spirit, which is the Word of God." I do this for myself and all of my family.

Father, I ask that You send forth Your angels to take charge over us as in Your Word in Psalms 91. All levels and forms of angels: ministering, warring, intercession, deliverance, messenger, impartation, reinforcement angels, armies of angels and all others we don't know about, I ask, commission, and release them, in Jesus' name!

We ask You to put a double hedge of protection around each of us so that no hurt, harm or danger will come near us physically, mentally, psychologically, emotionally and spiritually. When the enemy comes to attack us in any way, he will have to flee from us seven different ways, because he sees Your anointing, Your light, power and glory shining through us. We thank you Father for providing our needs and we lack nothing, according to Your riches and glory in Christ Jesus, exceedingly above more than we could ever ask or think. I choose to forgive my enemies and bless those who curse me and do wrong to me. I put them in Your hands, I release any offenses in the name of Jesus.

I thank You Father that I walk in favor because I am an heir to God, joint-heir with Christ Jesus. I thank you that I am blessed and highly favored. In Jesus name.

Psalm 91

Pray this daily

Security of the One Who Trusts in the LORD.

1 He who [a]dwells in the shelter of the Most High

Will remain secure *and* rest in the shadow of the Almighty

(whose power no enemy can withstand).

2 I will say of the LORD, "He is my refuge and my fortress,

My God, in whom I trust [with great confidence, and on

whom I rely]!"

3 For He will save you from the trap of the fowler,

And from the deadly pestilence.

4 He will cover you *and* completely protect you with His pinions,

And under His wings you will find refuge,

His faithfulness is a shield and a wall.

5 You will not be afraid of the terror of night,

Nor of the arrow that flies by day,

6 Nor of the pestilence that stalks in darkness,

Nor of the destruction (sudden death) that lays waste at noon.

7 A thousand may fall at your side

And ten thousand at your right hand,

But danger will not come near you.

8 You will only [be a spectator as you] look on with your eyes

And witness the (divine) repayment of the wicked (as you

watch safely from the shelter of the Most High).

9 Because you have made the LORD, (who is) my refuge,

Even the Most High, your dwelling place,

10 No evil will befall you,

Nor will any plague come near your tent.

11 For He will command His angels in regard to you,

To protect *and* defend *and* guard you in all your ways (of obedience and service).

12 They will lift you up in their hands,

So that you do not (even) strike your foot against a stone.

13 You will tread upon the lion and cobra,

The young lion and the serpent you will trample underfoot.

14 Because he set his love on Me, therefore I will save him,

I will set him [securely] on high, because he knows My

name [he confidently trusts and relies on Me, knowing

I will never abandon him, no, never].

15 "He will call upon Me, and I will answer him,

I will be with him in trouble,

I will rescue him and honor him.

16 "With a long life I will satisfy him

And I will let him see My salvation."

About the Author

Grace Cruz is an apostolic leader and a prophetic minister. Her mandate is to raise up women of all ages by bringing healing, deliverance, teaching and equipping to them to be all that God created them to be. Through Grace's gifting to minister healing and deliverance to the soul and to draw out gifts and callings in a person, through Divine wisdom, many have discovered their God-given destiny, resulting in a life that is transformed and equipped to do mighty exploits for God and to be carriers of His power and glory. Grace has a passion for intercession and spending time with the Lord in the 'secret place'.

Grace lives in Kaneohe, Hawaii, but is originally from Texas. Grace is a wife and a mother of three children and one grandchild. She lives in Hawaii with her husband and two daughters. Grace loves spending time with her family, going to the beach, hiking and exploring the islands.

Grace Cruz is founder of Grace Cruz Ministries, Kingdom Woman Arise, Int., and Esther Arise Youth Outreach. Grace is ordained and commissioned through Patricia King's Women In Ministry Network. Grace is 'in alignment' with Ryan LeStrange's Impact International Apostolic Fellowship.

Connect with Grace Cruz at

www.gracecruzministries.org

www.ingramcontent.com/pod-product-compliance
Lightning Source LLC
Chambersburg PA
CBHW051827090426
42736CB00011B/1687